D1535372

Oakland Community College
Orchard Ridge Campus Library
27055 Orchard Lake Road
Farmington, Michigan 48024

Rape of the American Virgins

Martin Luther King, Jr.
Learning Resources Center
Oakland Community College
Farmington, Michigan 48024

Presented by
Mr. & Mrs.
Carl Barton

ERRATUM

From the fourth line from the bottom of page 101 through line 2 of page 102, the text should read:

Shortly after Paiewonsky resigned, in February, 1969, the validity of the contract was questioned. After he took office, Governor Evans turned the matter over to the Department of the Interior for arbitration. The finding was that Halprin's charges were reasonable and that he was entitled to $68,750 in addition to the $171,875 that was paid before the contract was officially suspended. No lawsuit was filed against Lawrence Halprin.

ADDENDUM

On page 105, between "1967.*" and "According to the *Post*," in the sixth text line from the bottom of the page, the following sentence should appear:

The Justice Department cleared Udall of all conflict-of-interest charges.

Rape
of the
American
Virgins

EDWARD A. O'NEILL

PRAEGER PUBLISHERS
New York • Washington • London

HC
157
.V6
O5

CR 11/75

PRAEGER PUBLISHERS
111 Fourth Avenue, New York, N.Y. 10003, U.S.A.
5, Cromwell Place, London SW7 2JL, England

Published in the United States of America in 1972
by Praeger Publishers, Inc.

© 1972 by Praeger Publishers, Inc.

All rights reserved

Library of Congress Catalog Card Number: 72-189917

Printed in the United States of America

Contents

Acknowledgments

There are many people in the Virgin Islands—natives, continentals, foreigners, and "aliens"—to whom I owe large thanks for help in gathering the information for this book. Some are identified in these pages, some are not, but all were important to me. One who is not identified but who helped open my eyes to the place was John "Leif" Erickson of St. John, who died on April 9, 1972. The conclusions drawn and the impressions formed from the information supplied by all these people are my own. I thank Gladys Topkis for her cheerfully exact editorial help. And, for financial assistance that made my final research possible, I would like to thank the Stern Foundation's Fund for Investigative Journalism, as well as James Boyd, its secretary.

Rape of the American Virgins

1. Trouble in Paradise

A great many people have fallen in love with the American Virgins—with cause.

These storybook islands have a magical charm—in the beat of the steel drums, in a language with a Calypso lilt, in their history, and in their architecture. Seven flags have flown over the Virgin Islands—the Dutch, the Danish, the French, the Knights of Malta, the Spanish, the British, and the United States—and these influences are now interwoven in a distinctive cultural pattern to be found nowhere else in the world. From the sun-drenched beaches to the numerous misty mountain peaks, a visit to the Virgin Islands is an adventure one will never forget.

So says the introduction to *Our Caribbean Gems: The U.S. Virgin Islands,* a pamphlet of the Department of the Interior, and this claim by some unknown bureaucrat-lyricist is not unwarranted. In many ways it is as true today as it was when the department took over management of the islands from the U.S. Navy in 1931. Despite the deterioration apparent to any visitor who takes time off from bargain-shopping or daiquiri-drinking to look and smell and feel, the Virgins remain glorious. But they have been ravished. And they are in trouble.

Thus, on a typically lovely day in November, 1971, as soon as the skipper of the glass-bottomed boat had his mooring lines aboard, he began apologizing to his passengers—tourists off the Queen Elizabeth II, which has been putting into St. Thomas periodically since she began Caribbean cruising in the autumn of 1970. They would have to wait a bit to see the tropical fish and coral reef formation he had been telling them about.

"It's the pollution. But I'll get you out of this in a few minutes."

"This" was the slate-gray, stinking waters of Charlotte Amalie Harbor, a mile-wide, protected anchorage into which have sailed pirates and privateers, slavers and traders, and more recently five hundred cruise ships a year carrying a quarter of a million vacationing mainland Americans seeking fun and bargains. Three million gallons of raw sewage flow into the harbor each day, a by-product of the runaway development that has occurred on St. Thomas and the other U.S. Virgins in the past decade. The deplorable state of Charlotte Amalie Harbor, once clean and turquoise, where people could swim as recently as the early 1960s, belies the slogan on the territory's license plates: "American Paradise."

So do a lot of other excrescences that phenomenal growth has brought.

Since 1960, the population of the Virgin Islands—St. Thomas, St. Croix, and St. John—has more than doubled. The number of tourists—the lifeblood of the economy—has increased fivefold to more than a million a year. Government revenues have increased sixfold, to an annual take of well over $100 million. Other growth indicators have similarly zoomed during the past decade. Building permits have quadrupled. The number of business licenses has tripled. The value of new construction has increased eight times. And, since 1963, bank deposits have grown from $52 million to $648 million—an astounding increase of nearly 1,200 per cent.

Of course, there is still plenty to support the "Paradise" boast—the climate, "air-conditioned" by the tradewinds most of the year; breathtaking views from thousand-foot hills; the Caribbean (in Lafcadio Hearn's phrase, "absurdly, impossibly blue"), where the fishing is exciting and the sailing just about the best in the world; sunsets that are close to unforgettable; coral reefs, most of them still teeming with fish and sea life that even a novice snorkeler can enjoy; sun, surf, sand; the old Danish charm of the waterfronts and streets of Christiansted; the rain forest of St. Croix's north shore; jungle-covered plantation ruins on St. John; rum drinks on hotel verandahs high on St. Thomas's hillsides—all of these things wrapped in a West Indian ambiance as easy to slip into as a terry-cloth robe.

But the combination of economic growth and the islands' nearly incomparable assets has produced no Utopia. Instead, misused prosperity and uncontrolled growth have virtually blown the islands' chance of becoming what President John F. Kennedy wanted them to be: a "showcase of democracy." For the boom, far from helping to preserve the islands' attractions, which gave rise to it, has hurt them. Beaches have been mined for sand to build hotels and condominiums. Offshore dredging has damaged many of the literally irreplaceable reefs, and it is changing the character of the sea bottom so that waves and currents are cutting into existing beaches. After every rain—and it rains hard and often—the runoff from hillsides scarred by bulldozers for expensive homesites makes bays and coves look like mud puddles. New industries attracted to St. Croix by generous tax subsidies—an oil refinery and a bauxite-processing plant—emit more smoke, gases, and dust than the nearly constant tradewinds can carry away. Most roads leading out of the principal towns are lined with shack settlements only partly hidden by flowering vines and tropical foliage. In the towns, where there is no foliage, other shacks stand stark and depressing and out in the open, many only a block or so away from the "duty-free" shops filled with luxuries from all over the world. The road system is unbelievably bad: A federal Bureau of Public Roads study made in 1969 found that 70 per cent of the roads were unsafe for speeds higher than 30 miles an hour, and 31 per cent for speeds higher than 20 miles an hour. (Compounding the danger is the astonishing anomaly that on the bad roads and narrow town streets some twenty thousand motor vehicles, virtually all of them designed for driving on the right side of the road, are being driven on the left, as in Britain.)

How did it all go wrong so fast?

I began asking myself this question not long after my first, temporarily dazzling sight of the islands in the summer of 1970. Like every other visitor, I was initally overwhelmed at the prospect (seen from a jet-plane window) of the "misty mountain peaks" rising from the translucent sea. But the first impression didn't hold—as I was to learn it does not for many visitors. There are too many scars, too much that is shoddy, too many almost immediately apparent problems. In five months' residence on the islands, where I had gone to do a free-lance job, I saw much more that was wrong. Public services and public facilities of all kinds are inadequate be-cause little attempt has been made to keep up with burgeon-ing development. The school system is distressingly bad, with 18,000 students crowded into inadequate classrooms with inadequate textbooks and equipment. Those who can afford it—white and black—send their children to private secular or parochial schools. These children, numbering 6,000, make up a quarter of the Virgin Islands school enroll-ment. Health facilities are inadequate, and medical person-nel are critically scarce; when there is a crisis—an explosion or an airliner crash—doctors and nurses have to be flown in from Puerto Rico to help out. Telephone and electrical services are erratic. A Washington consultant sent to the islands by the Department of the Interior in 1961 testily reported that there were two "outages" (power failures) during the ten days he spent on the islands. Eleven years later, "outages" still occur about once a week.

Instead of using its sudden prosperity to meet these and other inadequacies, the Virgin Islands government chose instead to put its citizens on the public payroll—more than 7,700 of them. Their salaries and wages amount to more than 70 per cent of the government's operating expenses. With so many Virgin Islanders in government jobs, outside labor has to be imported to fill the jobs created by the boom. Virtually all of these outsiders are blacks from "down-island"—the British, French, and Dutch West Indies. With their families, these aliens form a community of perhaps 20,000 and place severe strain on the social fabric of the islands. For the native Virgin Islander resents the aliens' presence—as he resents the need for their presence. The native also resents the new whites from the mainland attracted by the boom, some of whom —the artisans and technicians—form a kind of "redneck" community whose prejudices cause problems especially bothersome in a place where racial unease previously was rare. And, lastly, the native resents the tourists—although at the same time he knows that they are vital to the islands' well-being. (Anyone who has seen Charlotte Amalie's Main Street when four or five cruise ships are in the harbor and two or three thousand curiously dressed passengers are elbowing their way from shop to shop can understand the resentment.) The Virgin Islands government meanwhile keeps up a cheerful advertising campaign designed to make the native more friendly to visitors.

"The only trouble," a native shopkeeper said, "is that the tourist is here for fun, for a party. We're here all the time, and nobody can be in a happy-happy party mood all the time."

One of the hundreds of people I have talked to about what went wrong when prosperity came to these islands, which a

President of the United States once called an "effective poor-house," is a man who first became enamored of the American Virgins during World War II when he ran agricultural co-operatives in Puerto Rico and the Virgins for the Department of Agriculture. Readers old enough to remember the halcyon days of radio may recall him, the voice of the old National Farm and Home Hour ("It's a beautiful day in Chicago . . ."). Connie B. Gay, who made a fortune in independent broadcasting, built a house on a St. Thomas hillside overlooking the sea and became a legal resident—a "continental," as residents originally from the mainland are called. Over the years, he watched the islands develop and saw other mainlanders come to visit, then, like him, return to establish themselves as Virgin Islanders.

Gay, who is now a resident of McLean, Virginia, might have played a larger role in the islands' story than he did, had it not been for the influence, at the opening of the 1960s, of old friendships on new politics. That story belongs in another chapter of this book. He is introduced here only as an example of the people who fell in love with the American Virgins—and one who is especially outspoken about what went wrong.

My inquiries turned up evidence of many officials and others who understood what damage was being done to the "American Paradise" and who tried, ineffectually, to prevent it. But, on the whole, the influx of developers and entrepreneurs, agents of this corporation or that holding company, officials of the Department of the Interior and other government agencies, members of Congress and their staffs, did not breed a climate of reform. The atmosphere was more sky's-the-limit, what's-in-it-for-me-Jack. Connie B. Gay characterized it vividly: "The practice when big wheels came down was to meet them at the airport, where there would be drinks and then they would be taken off to Mountain Top. 'You've got to have a banana daiquiri and enjoy the view.' Banana daiquiris go down real good, and after a couple of them, things look a little different than they did. Then it would be off to a fancy estate where there would be more booze and pussy wall to wall. When you combine booze and broads and that Virgin Islands moon looking down and maybe a steel band playing down below the verandah, your point-of-view changes. It would seduce a preacher, and maybe the Pope would even throw away his Bible."

There is no doubt that this transfer of the islands' traditional carnival spirit to governmental and commercial purposes is one of the reasons why what could have developed as an American Eden has come close to turning into a snake pit. But, as this book seeks to show, it's only one factor among many in the long story of rapacious dealings that began even before Europeans sailed into the sea named for the Caribs, that fierce tribe of Indians who cruised up from South America, took a liking to the real estate, and ate the original inhabitants.

2. Cannibals and Other Colonials

The origin of the island chain to which the American Virgins belong goes back more than a hundred million years. Even then, the sea-encircled mountaintops were thrust upward as part of a process that had itself begun still another hundred million years earlier, when the crust of the adolescent earth was rent apart and the portions that became North and South America moved away from Europe and Africa, forming the Atlantic Ocean. A glance at the world map shows that the coastlines of the Western Hemisphere and the Eastern Hemisphere could roughly be fitted together, jigsaw-puzzle fashion, were it not for the Gulf of Mexico and the Caribbean. These expanses of water make it look as if some of the puzzle's pieces had fallen under the table. What probably happened is that sideslips, warps, bucklings, and undersea over-ridings occurred as the moving continental plates of enormous mass shifted slowly into place. The end result was the present-day oceanic mountain chain, the real height of which is Himalayan (the Croix Deep between St. Thomas and St. Croix plunges 20,713 feet below the surface, and the Atlantic's Puerto Rican Trench, not too far from the Virgins, is more than 27,500 feet deep).

The arc of the islands and the sea around them are still unfinished geologically. Mild earthquakes occur now and then, and there are some active volcanoes, like Mount Pelée on Martinique, which in 1902 produced one of the greatest explosions in history, killing thirty thousand people. The mechanics of the earth's surface and the ocean's bottom in the area continue to operate much as they did during earlier epochs, and no geologist worth his rock hammer would be so brash as to predict what might occur in the way of seismic activity in the Caribbean in the near or even distant future. One I wrote to, a man who had recently vacationed in the Virgins, surprised me, however, with a sociological obiter dictum tacked to the geological information I asked for: "The islands' turbulent geologic history is almost a prophetic backdrop to the social upheavals that have beset the area, upheavals that in the future may be less patient but no less dynamic than those of the recent, and the prehistoric, past."

The Virgins are not only volcanic but also sit uneasily in hurricane country. Although there have been no storms of major proportions for the past thirty years, there is an island memory of devastating winds that every July sends the superstitious and the devout to special services on "Supplication Day" to pray that the storms will not strike. In October, the months of danger having safely passed, they celebrate "Hurricane Thanksgiving."

The point should not be stretched too far—all islands in all the world's seas give their residents a sense of trouble lurking that cannot be walked away from—but even the geology and meteorology of the Virgins seem to hint of threat. Their history speaks rather more plainly. And here the disasters, with few exceptions, are prophetically manmade rather than natural.

*   *   *

Washington Irving, in his *Life and Voyages of Christopher Columbus,* observed that the explorer seemed to have had an inexhaustible store of names for places he discovered. On his second voyage to the New World, the Genoese adventurer had to dig again and again into his name bag. His second attempt to find "the Indies" had taken him much farther south than did his first voyage of discovery. Coming down the northeast tradewinds that blow almost constantly from the islands off Africa across 3,500 miles of Atlantic, on November 3, 1493, he discovered the necklace of large and small islands, rocks, islets, and cays that geographers and yachtsmen now know as the Lesser Antilles. Unlike the low-lying Bahamas, scene of Columbus's first landfall, they would have been hard to miss. It is likely that landfall on the second voyage was made many miles at sea, for the first sighting was of an island rising more than 4,600 feet. Columbus named it Dominica.

Leaving behind the dark Atlantic, Columbus took his cockleshell fleet of seventeen ships, caravels, and pinnaces through Dominica Passage into the ever-changing blue waters of the Caribbean. We have no information about his impressions, but even the singleminded "Admiral of the Ocean Sea" must have been exalted by the sweep of high-rising islands stretching to the north and northwest horizons. He paused briefly at Guadeloupe, which, in the manner of more modern explorers, he named for a sponsor—the monastery of the Virgin of Guadeloupe had given him help in his early, struggling days in Spain. Leaving Guadeloupe, where his men found gory evidence of cannibalism, he coasted the chain of islands, naming them as he went—Montserrat, Antigua, Nevis, St. Christopher. St. Bartholomew, St. Martin.

On the fourteenth day of Caribbean sailing, Irving says, "the weather proving boisterous," Columbus anchored his fragile fleet in the protection of what is now Salt Bay on the northern shore of the island he called Santa Cruz. (The name became St. Croix, pronounced "Croy," during the seventeenth-century period of French ownership.) A boat was put ashore for water and reconnaissance. The landing party found a village, virtually deserted save for a few women and boys who, according to an early chronicle, "were mostly captives from other islands." The Spaniards also found, as they had in Guadeloupe, piles of human bones and a few parts of bodies hanging to dry. On the way back to the anchored ships, the landing party encountered a canoe loaded with Carib Indians—including two women—who, at the astounding sight of the Spaniards, turned and fled, laying down a barrage of arrows behind them. Columbus's men managed to ram the canoe with their boat, but the Caribs continued to fight, "discharging their arrows while swimming as dextrously as they had been on firm land."

Probably a little shaken by the ferocity of the Caribs' reactions—the first native American attempt to protect the neighborhood—Columbus moved out of Salt Bay on a northerly course into open water. "Soon," Irving says, "he came in sight of a great cluster of islands, some verdant and covered with forests, but the greater part naked and sterile, rising into rugged mountains with rocks of bright azure color and some of glistening white. These, with his usual vivacity of imagination, he supposed to contain rich minerals and precious stones."

And here Columbus let his vivacious imagination have its head. This closely knit group of some fifty small islands (uninhabited, according to the captain of a caravel sent to investigate) he named *Santa Ursula y las once mille virgines,* thereby setting in train thousands of what used to be called "off-color" jokes. Today, visitors to the U.S. possession can buy T-shirts bearing the slogan "I SLEPT ON A VIRGIN (island)."

The Catholic Encyclopedia says that St. Ursula probably was a Roman, but legend, which is more fun, says that she was a fourth-century Celtic princess who led 11,000 virgins from Britain on a pilgrimage to Rome. The homeward journey took the group to the banks of the Rhine near what is now Cologne, where they encountered an army of invading Huns who took them captive and ultimately slaughtered them.

* * *

The earliest inhabitants of the Virgins, as evidenced by their artifacts, were Arawaks, an Indian tribal people from the South American mainland who had been forced up the island chain by tougher neighbors, penetrating as far as Cuba and, some say, even southern Florida. The Arawaks were savages Rousseau would have liked: The adjective almost universally used by writers to describe them is "gentle," and their life-style can be construed from the invention they left behind them—the hammock.

The drying flesh that Columbus's landing parties found in the Carib settlements on St. Croix and Guadeloupe probably was Arawakan. The word "cannibal," by etymological byways, comes from "Carib," and it is said that Caribs used to keep captive Arawaks like livestock for slaughter. The Caribs, also originally from South America, were not nearly the equals of the Polynesians in their sea movements, but their canoes (another Carib word) were far-ranging, and in them they were known to have raided Puerto Rico. Beset by Caribs on the south and west, the gentle Arawaks were doomed to fall before the Spanish Conquest. Unlike the Indians of the United States later, they had no place to move on to, even for a time. Within a century of the discovery of America, the Arawaks were extinct. But for some rock carvings, shards of pottery, and the backyard hammock they left us, they are scarcely remembered today.

* * *

For most of the century after Columbus's departure, the Virgin Islands, like the rest of the Lesser Antilles, slept under the tropical sun. The tradewinds blew, as they had for millennia. Now and then, hurricanes uprooted lignum vitae and mahogany trees and flattened the tangled jungle growth. An occasional earthquake shook the hillsides, where no one came to look for "mines of rich minerals and precious stones." The Spaniards may at times have put in from nearby Puerto Rico or from Hispaniola, seeking Carib Indians for slaves, but the Caribs apparently moved down the chain to the vicinity of Dominica, where a very few of their descendants can still be found. Not until the rise of nationalism and mercantilism in Europe and the nearly ceaseless wars of the sixteenth and seventeenth centuries did adventurers other than the Spaniards look to the Caribbean.

Then, even before the defeat of the Spanish Armada, marauding raiders flying Dutch, French, and British ensigns began to appear in the West Indies, taking Spanish treasure as they came across it. The best-known of their commanders, Sir Francis Drake, raided Panama and sacked Cartagena. Tradition says that he visited the Virgins at about this time. On St. Thomas, overlooking Pillsbury Sound, a strategic passage between the Atlantic and the Caribbean, there is a site known as "Drake's Seat," where Sir Francis was supposed to have watched for Spanish ship movements. The story probably is myth, but it is certain that Drake did move a fleet through the sound in 1595 and used St. Thomas as a resting place for his troops before an unsuccessful attack on San Juan, Puerto Rico, after which *geste* he died of unheroic dysentery. Three years later, the Earl of Cumberland, following a similar course to a successful raid on San Juan, stopped in the Virgins and reported the islands to be unpopulated.

With the waning of Spanish power, and as the sixteenth century turned into the seventeenth, the feisty, newly independent Dutch began large-scale operations in the Caribbean. Salt was the treasure they were after. Because Portugal had united with the Netherlands' former oppressor and enemy, Spain, the Dutch had lost the vital salt trade they had carried on, in monopolistic fashion, with Portugal. They had to go to extraordinary lengths to revive it. Off the coast of Venezuela, 5,000 miles from Amsterdam, was a peculiar coastal formation that produced an enormous salt pan which was known to Dutch captains and seized upon as a substitute for the Portuguese source. Between 1600 and 1605, ten Dutch ships a month were arriving at the salt source to get the precious substance needed for the fish trade at home and the preservation of meat in a large part of northern Europe.

In this same period, the Caribbean became more and more an arena for competing continental attempts at settlement. Among the early adventurer-imperialists was Sir Walter Raleigh—who, after his North Carolina experience, should have known better. Raleigh tried to colonize the fever-ridden coast of Guiana, his widely proclaimed "El Dorado." The French, urged on by the ambitions of Louis XIII and his counselors Richelieu and Mazarin, also came into the southerly islands. But settlement proved more difficult than raiding Spanish treasure galleons or even mining salt. The first attempt of the British at settlement, on St. Lucia in 1605, was repulsed by the still-formidable Caribs, and a second attempt, on Grenada, was turned away by the same tribe. The British were not able to set up shop until 1623 (and then on the relatively inconsequential island of Nevis), three years after their Pilgrim compatriots on the *Mayflower* had come to Plymouth Rock. The Dutch and French had problems similar to the British, but by the middle years of the seventeenth century all were settled down as colonialists—to the great discomfiture of Spain. Over the years, the interlopers' holdings varied, depending on who had been successful in what war, but many of them were as they are today: the Dutch on Aruba, Curacao, and Bonaire; the French on Martinique and Guadeloupe; the British on Barbados, Nevis, St. Kitt's, and Antigua. But the islands called the Virgins still remained unpossessed, despite the magnificent and protected harbor of the one that somebody had named St. Thomas. (Why one of Ursula's girls was given a masculine saint's name is a mystery.) The lack of habitation may have been the result of the islands' proximity to Puerto Rico, from which even a weakened Spain could have struck with force against settlement by any outsider. The place was well known, and roving Danish captains frequently found shelter in the bowl-like harbor, but the steep hills around it were empty of life except for darting, bright birds and scampering lizards.

*　*　*

Denmark, the smallish peninsula known today mostly for its dairy products and tourist attractions, was, during the Age of Exploration and Discovery, *the* power in northwestern Europe. The Danes controlled the entrance to the Baltic and held effective hegemony over Norway, Sweden, and parts of northern Germany. They also had continental ambitions that got them into disastrous troubles with Sweden, which shook the Danish overlordship after 1523, and into six years of the Thirty Years' War, which cost them a lot more territory. But the Danes were outreaching seamen as well. They joined in the search for the Holy Grail of the period—the Northwest Passage—and even ventured as far as India, where in the early 1600s they set up "factories" near Calcutta and on the Coromandel Coast that remained active until the early years of England's Queen Victoria's reign. Through their connections with the energetic Dutch, Danish merchants and ship captains looked westward to the Caribbean.

As early as 1625, a Danish West India company was formed in Copenhagen—by a Dutchman. It never got beyond the paper state, and Danish involvement in the area did not come to much beyond trading voyages by individual ships until after 1670, when the British and the Spanish, in one of the many treaties they were always signing in those days, more or less opened settlement on the islands of the Caribbean for all comers. That year, what apparently was a group of court insiders in Copenhagen organized a second Danish West India company with one Frederick Gyldenlove, an illegitimate son of King Christian V, as its president. A charter was issued on March 11, 1671, and a decision made to settle on St. Thomas. A little more than eight months later, the Company had two ships fitted out and on their way to the Caribbean.

One of the ships had to turn back, but the other, the *Pharoah,* made the tedious winter passage to the Cape Verde Islands off the African coast, caught the tradewinds, and set course for the Lesser Antilles. On board were 166 indentured servants, 61 convicts, and a remarkably small crew of 12, all under the command of the Company's first governor, George Iversen, a thirty-three-year-old seaman who had first sailed to the Caribbean as a boy of thirteen. On May 25, 1672, more than six months after she had set out, the *Pharoah* sailed into the harbor of St. Thomas. It had been a horrendous voyage, for of the 239 who had boarded the ship in Copenhagen, 86 were dead or would be dead within a few weeks—victims of scurvy and other diseases brought on by the unbelievably primitive living conditions of ships of that day. (At that, the proportion of casualties on the *Pharoah* was not high compared to the rate on some later ships. The *Pelican,* with 62 persons aboard, sailed from Copenhagen in November, 1672; 7 died at sea and 53 others shortly after arrival in St. Thomas. Another ship, the *Merman,* lost 34 of the 58 persons it carried.)

Iversen took little time out to mourn the *Pharoah's* dead, setting the survivors immediately to work clearing land for the town that he named Charlotte Amalie, after Christian V's queen. (In these days of air conditioning and power-driven machinery of all kinds, it is painful to imagine what it must have been like for Iversen's transplanted northern Europeans, accustomed as they were to cold winters and the timid but benign sun of the Baltic, to tackle tropical jungle in enervating heat and humidity with only crude hand tools. They did not even have the help of draft animals.) He soon discovered, as the British had before him, that convicts would not work except under harsh discipline and close supervision, and wrote to the Company directors, "They are uncontrollable fellows whom neither the workhouse nor the penitentiary could improve." The bonded laborers were scarcely better, and Iversen even had trouble with the clergy sent out by the official Lutheran Church. The first minister to survive (one died on shipboard and a second shortly after arrival) caused the governor so much trouble that he had to be sent home. Back in Copenhagen, the minister sued the Company for damages; the Company filed a counter-suit charging him with drunkenness on the job. The minister argued: "It was a state easily brought about by the terrible stuff they make in that land." He may have had a point. The local tipple was unaged rum known as "kill-devil."

"Kill-devil" was not an export item, for very little sugar was grown in St. Thomas before the early eighteenth century. The principal money crop at first was tobacco, poorly suited to the climate but much desired back home. Iversen levied fines in units of hundreds of pounds of tobacco to get the settlers to turn out for militia drills and as punishment for crimes, misdemeanors, and other civic failings. The system must have been reasonably effective, for Iversen managed to build a fort, to survey and allot plantations, and to get together enough tobacco, cotton, indigo, and dyewoods to send a ship back to Denmark every now and then. But the cargoes were small, principally because there were so few settlers. Replacements were sent out, but they kept dying. Despite a steady stream leaving Copenhagen, there were only

156 whites on St. Thomas in 1679, Iversen's last year as governor—and many of these people were British and Dutch drifters and Huguenots from the French West Indies, who even in the distant Caribbean had been affected by Louis XIV's revocation of the Edict of Nantes.

There were, in addition, 176 black slaves, the first of whom had come to the island through shipwreck in 1673.

* * *

The introduction of African slaves into the Caribbean probably was inevitable, with burgeoning European markets clamoring for sugar, tobacco, cotton, and other hot-climate products and looking to the relatively convenient West Indies as a source of supply. Repeated attempts to develop the islands' rich potential with white indentured labor and convicts were unsuccessful. Strange fevers and the climate killed off an astonishing number of them. (A sizable portion of the few who had survived fled their bonds as soon as they saw a chance to become privateers, pirates, or merely free men on nearby islands where no questions were asked.) Northern European entrepreneurs turned, as the Spaniards had done before them, to the West Coast of Africa as a source of manpower supposedly inured to the equatorial sun.

There is an awful irony about the way the Spaniards first came to use black slave labor in the West Indies. In the early sixteenth century, a monk, Bartolomeo de Las Casas, appalled by the effects of forced labor on the indigenous Arawakan Indians of Puerto Rico, recommended to the Spanish authorities that black Africans, accustomed, so the monk thought, to arduous work, be substituted. The idea was taken up with enthusiasm, and thousands of blacks were forcibly brought from Africa to the Spanish possessions. Like many humanitarian reformers, de Las Casas came to have second thoughts about his suggestion, for the condition of the Arawaks did not markedly improve, and the conditions imposed on the blacks were dreadful. He appealed again and again to Madrid to stop the traffic, and was still appealing when he died in Yucatan as a bishop of the church.

Considering the extent of their New World possessions, the Spaniards did not import an enormous number of slaves. Unhampered by any latter-day de Las Casas on the mainland of South and Central America and Mexico, they usually made wide use of indigenous people to build their American Empire. They also did not, in any large way, engage in the slave trade, that being in the early years one of the specialities of Portugal. But after the Netherlands broke away from Spanish domination, the hard-driving Dutch, always with an eye for profit, moved into the slave business, in which they were to hold a predominant position until the early eighteenth century. (A Dutch privateer brought the first slaves to Virginia in 1619, landing twenty of them, captured from the Portuguese, at Jamestown.) But the other European nations decided that the trade was too profitable to be left to the Dutch. At one time, about 1670, there were nine nations and forty-three chartered companies operating slave factories on the West African coast. The insatiable demands of the West Indian plantations attracted slave-traders from England, France, Denmark, Sweden, the German principality of Brandenburg, and even Latvia (Courlanders). Between 1680 and 1786, more than 2,130,000 slaves were landed in the British West Indies. Since the deaths of slaves on the hideous "Middle Passage" of the triangular rum-slaves-sugar trade ranged from 10 to 55 per cent, the original number loaded on the African coast for the British plantations alone may have exceeded three million.

The Baltic Brandenburgers, subjects of the Hohenzollern "Great Elector," Frederick William, were relatively unsuccessful in the slave trade—as well as in their alternative occupation, privateering—until the financially strapped Danish West Indian Company in 1686 rented a St. Thomas plantation to them. With a West Indian base, and operating from Africa's Guinea Coast, the Brandenburgers began shipping slaves by the hundreds. Their success at first bred envy among the Danes, but as time went on it was followed by active harassment and restrictions of the plantation's operations on St. Thomas. The Brandenburgers' essays into colonialism lasted less than thirty years. Danish interference, pressure from investors and the government at home, and victimization by pirates and privateers proved too much for even Prussian single-mindedness. The Great Elector's son, King Frederick I, a notorious penny-pincher, closed out the Caribbean operation in 1715, and Prussian dreams of overseas fleets and colonies died, not to be revived until the days of Bismarck. However, the Brandenburger legacy in the Virgins, the slave trade, was one the Danes were to take up and build with gusto.

* * *

Most of the developments in the slave trade came several years after Iversen's stay as governor. The few slaves on St. Thomas scarcely presaged the lucrative future of the Charlotte Amalie market. Iversen had other problems. To use a still-favorite St. Thomian word, he was a harassed (pronounced "horaced") man. Earnest and hardworking as he must have been, he still could not cope with the enormously difficult problems common to all colonial settlements of the period. Lacking substantial support from his directors (who had expected to grow rich from their Caribbean scheme), beset by complaints from the planters, constantly fearful that the nearby Spaniards or British might decide to toss him and the rest of the Danes out, tired of the rotting heat, he gave up in 1679 and asked permission to come home.

A succession of extraordinary rascals, apparently chosen more for their connections and glibness than for their competence, followed Iversen. The first three of these worthies were jailed at one time or another, and one of them was eventually beheaded for his behavior. This trio ran the island for nearly a decade and, taking advantage of Denmark's neutrality in European struggles for power, made St. Thomas a haven for privateers, pirates, and shady operators from all parts of the West Indies. Money was made, lots of it, but not from the plantations and not for the island treasury. Describing this period, Waldemar Westergaard, the Danish-American historian, wrote: "Of dividends there had been no thought. The stockholders could count themselves fortunate that the island was still under Danish sovereignty."

The first of these rascals was Nicholas Esmit. After a year or so of his misgovernment and mismanagement, the unhappy Company sent Iversen back to replace him, but early in the voyage convicts on board mutinied and threw Iversen and most of the ship's complement overboard. Nicholas's brother Adolph, aided by his attractive wife's connections in court, talked himself into the job, and when he replaced his brother in Charlotte Amalie sent him back to Denmark to jail. During Adolph's tenure, pirates, then at the height of their power in the Caribbean, came and went through the protecting arms of St. Thomas's harbor with apparent impunity, and some writers of the day say that Adolph Esmit himself engaged in piratical activities.

The British, who held the nearby islands to the southwest, were particularly put out by Esmit's *laissez-faire* and protested to him time and again about his tolerance of piracy. On one occasion, an exasperated British captain entered Charlotte Amalie Harbor and burned a notorious French pirate ship while its captain, Jean Hamlin, and most of his crew were ashore enjoying the amenities the island offered. In the midst of the operation a cannonball was fired at the British warship from the fort where Esmit had his headquarters. The following morning the governor apologized; the shot, he said, had "merely been a salute." The exasperated

British conveyed their unhappiness about Esmit and his free-and-easy operations to Copenhagen, and in 1684 the Company sent out another governor.

The new man, Gabriel Milan, seems to have been the most devious and erratic of the lot. He talked the Danish government into giving him a proper warship to make the voyage to St. Thomas—not some tired Caribbean-trade tub —and took with him his wife and family, a cargo of fine wines, and six dogs. Also on board was a young clerk named John Lorentz, a seventeenth-century organization man who was later to become governor, and who appears to have been a Company spy. Milan stopped first at Nevis, a British island 150 miles from St. Thomas, to pay his respects to the governor, whom he sought to mollify by taking a sizable British delegation along to Charlotte Amalie to participate in his inaugural festivities. For ten days, Milan lavishly entertained his British guests and the St. Thomas planters, ending the gala with a distribution of gifts to the Britishers. But when the new governor went to the treasury to pay the bill, he found it empty and had to borrow money from the planters he had just entertained. He thereupon threw Adolph Esmit in jail.

Considering the special treatment Milan had received from the Company and the Danish government, it is apparent that he was a man who made a considerable impression. But something happened to him in the tropics. Once in control in St. Thomas, he not only allowed the wide-open extralegal activities to continue but treated the planters and other residents with harshness unusual even for that day, using the jail and other punishments to get what he wanted from them. Possibly on information from Lorentz, the Company sent out a naval attorney, Michael Mikkelsen, to look into what was happening. When Mikkelsen, in February, 1686, walked into Milan's rooms in Charlotte Amalie's Christianfort, he found the governor "surrounded by firearms" and railing about the iniquities of the planters. Governor Milan was sent immediately to Mikkelsen's ship in the harbor and taken back to Denmark—together with Adolph Esmit, who had been in jail all the while. Milan was tried for various misdeeds and executed (punishment for bureaucratic misbehavior was rougher in those days than it is now), and only his family's pleadings to the King prevented the final ignominy of public exhibition of his head impaled on a stake.

Despite bad experiences with their appointees, a large degree of Danish permissiveness seems to have persisted among the Company's directors. No one else of experience being handy to run St. Thomas after Milan's execution, Adolph Esmit, released from his second jailing in Copenhagen through his wife's efforts, was again sent out as governor. But this time a vice-admiral went along to keep an eye on him. Esmit lasted exactly fifty-nine days before the admiral decided there had been no reform and sent him home. *Pro tem* governors then ran the place for two years until the Company, in near despair, rented the island to a supposedly canny Bergen merchant for ten years. After four years of failure, nonpayment of rent, and loss of fortune by the merchant, the Company in 1694 took back control.

Then finally, in the same year, after fourteen years of frustration and failure, the Danish West India Company came up with a winner. It chose the man in the gray flannel doublet, John Lorentz, sometime clerk, bookkeeper, possible Company spy, and briefly acting governor, to run its affairs in St. Thomas. Lorentz had learned over the years the secrets of being a successful "branch manager": Keep the home office only as informed as you want it to be but happy and obviously thought about. He communicated with Copenhagen frequently—and fulsomely. For example, a salutation he used on one letter was "High and Wellborn, so also Well-Noble Honorable Messrs Managers and Highly Favored Sirs." Who but a born cynic could resist such blandishments?

Lorentz was much more than a corporate politician, however. He was an imaginative doer. After watching the Brandenburgers for a few months, during which they brought in more than a thousand slaves, he wrote home: "Since all other trade is nothing compared to the slave trade, we should take it up at once." The Company for some years before had been half-heartedly engaged in the trade but had rented its African station to another merchant, who, like the renter of St. Thomas, also failed. Now, catching something of Lorentz's enthusiasm, the Company took back its African station and within a few years was sending a stream of carefully chosen blacks—Ibos, Mandingos, Fulanis, Kalibaris, and representatives of other proud tribes still important in Africa—across the sea to St. Thomas. Emphasis, at Lorentz's insistence, was on quality, and St. Thomas soon earned a reputation—terrible in retrospect, but proud and profitable then—for high-class merchandise. Buyers from as far away as Dutch Curaçao, off the coast of Venezuela, and the Carolinas swarmed into Charlotte Amalie Harbor, where they would board the slave ships and maul men, women, and children, looking for the best specimens. The careful colonials on St. Thomas, while making money on the traffic, also managed to keep the fittest slaves for themselves. (Today, the walk and style of the elegant, slim-hipped, broad-shouldered native St. Thomian bespeaks his elite ancestry.)

With a dependable labor force available, Lorentz turned his attention to production. He persuaded the planters to put their land into sugar cane, known as "white gold" in those days, instead of the tobacco and cotton they had been raising. (The importance the European colonial nations put on sugar is tellingly demonstrated by the fact that the Dutch gave up New Amsterdam so that they could keep Curaçao and the French, after defeats by the British, gave up Canada for Guadeloupe.) Although St. Thomas, with its steeply rising hills and chancy rainfalls, was by no means ideally suited to sugar cultivation, the enormous profits to be made with plentiful slave labor produced a quick revolution in the island's agriculture. By the time Lorentz died in 1702 (on the job, a management man to the end), terraces, built with what must have been incredible difficulty, climbed the volcanic hillsides as high as eight hundred feet above the sea. More planters came in, and more slaves. The population of St. Thomas three years before Lorentz took over as governor was 944—389 whites and 555 black slaves; by 1715, the population was 3,589, of whom 3,042 were slaves. The Danish West India Company was at last in business, and business was so good it decided to expand.

*   *   *

The first expansion was to St. John, an island roughly similar to St. Thomas in terrain, which lies only four miles across Pillsbury Sound, through which Drake had sailed. The Danes had tried to settle St. John in 1688 but were ejected by the British, who held the easterly group of Columbus's Virgins and the other islands farther along the chain. In 1717, however, one of Lorentz's successors as governor, Eric Bredal, decided to try settlement again and in secrecy built a fort on St. John. There was no apparent demurrer from the British. It could be that they were tired, having just finished fighting in the Caribbean extension of the War of the Spanish Succession, but it is more probable that, with other and more productive islands, they decided that St. John was not worth bothering about. The Danes took advantage of British inaction, and within fifteen years after Bredal built his fort there were 109 plantations on the island, most of them in sugar. Its population was 1,295—more than the number of permanent residents in 1960.

"Explosive" expansion of the Virgins, however, did not come until the Company bought St. Croix from the French in 1733. Between 1625 and 1675, the British, Dutch, Spaniards, French, and even the Knights of Malta had tried to develop the place, but all had given up. The Danes, within two years after purchase, had laid out 375 plantations on the island's eighty-five square miles of territory. St. Croix became a true "sugar island" and was to remain one past the middle of the twentieth century.

In its first forty years of Danish rule, St. Croix grew to be the home and, for the overwhelming majority of them, toiling place of 21,809 people living on estates with such names as Eliza's Retreat, Catherine's Rest, Anna's Hope, Upper Love, Lower Love, Jealousy, Whim, and Wheel of Fortune. On these fancifully named estates, the workers outnumbered planters and managers and the Company's administrators about twenty to one.

Like their fellow whites throughout the West Indies, the Europeans on the Virgin Islands lived in constant fear of slave revolt, and their government devised cruel and dreadful punishments to cow the blacks: pinching with red-hot tongs, amputation of ears, feet, and legs (but seldom hands, for that ruined a slave's utility), the lash, and, at last resort, hanging. Nonetheless, there were desperate uprisings. In 1733, the year settlement spread to St. Croix, slaves on St. John got into the fort on a ruse, killed all of the garrison save one soldier, destroyed or damaged half of the plantations on the island, and managed to hold out against the government and planters for six months before being overcome. It took the assistance of French troops from Martinique to end the rebellion. On burgeoning St. Croix in 1740, there was an uprising savagely put down with the assistance of "free coloreds" who formed a large part of the militia, and another abortive one in 1759 that was betrayed by black informers.

Despite black unrest, the Virgins grew and made progress. Having early learned its lesson, Denmark remained neutral in Europe's wars until the time of Napoleon and, as battling fleets struggled for control of the Caribbean in largely unorganized conflict, the entrepreneurs on the Virgins made money from all comers. (Parry and Sherlock, in their *Short History of the West Indies,* list thirteen European wars of the eighteenth and nineteenth centuries that spread into the area.) The feckless Danish West India Company, however, profited little from the benefits of neutrality. The general low level of its administrators—except John Lorentz—plus large-scale British and American colonial involvement in the quality slave trade, a succession of poor crop years, and fiscal incompetence (borrowing at high interest on low net income) finally brought the Company to the wall. In 1754, facing bankruptcy, it was bought out by King Frederick V.

Additional factors in the Company's failure were absentee ownership and the exploitation (then as now) of the islands' mercantile and physical resources by outsiders. Except in the early years of settlement, the majority of the population—and the people who made most of the money—were non-Danish, generally Dutch and British. Even the common language of the islands was not Danish but English, the trading *lingua franca* of the West Indies (the slaves spoke Dutch Creole). The islands' first newspaper, started in 1770, was called the *Royal Danish American Gazette,* but it was printed in English. Outsiders—Dutch, British, Scots, Irish, and German—managed the plantations and, more importantly, dominated trade. And it was a sizable trade. *The World Displayed,* a kind of eighteenth-century *Reader's Digest* of voyages and travels, described St. Thomas in 1769 as a "great resort of French, English, and Dutch vessels" where, "though a prodigious deal of business is transacted in time of peace, in time of war it is vastly increased, for being a neutral port, the privateers of all nations resort thither to sell their prizes."

These observations were made five years after the Danish government opened the harbor of Charlotte Amalie as a free port for intracolonial trade—a freedom extended in 1815 to trade with Europe and elsewhere. The free-port status was maintained throughout the years of Danish rule and still profoundly influences the Virgin Islands' economy.

*   *   *

By the beginning years of the nineteenth century, commerce overwhelmingly dominated the affairs of St. Thomas, and the population grew to meet the needs of the marketplace—jumping from 4,793 in 1796 to 14,022 in 1835. By 1835, nearly four fifths of St. Thomas's labor force, black and white, was working in support of trade. The whites were the importers, managers, merchants, brokers, and clerks; the blacks were the carpenters, sailmakers, shipwrights, boatmen, mechanics, warehousemen, and dock laborers. Nearly half of these blacks—about six thousand—were "free coloreds," for over the years there had been a slow but constant change in status among those of African descent. Many slaves bought their freedom with money earned on their days off or from the sale of things they grew or made. In addition, as in all colonial places where white women were scarce, there were thousands of children born to white fathers and slave mothers of varying hues, children who were given free status at birth. The total number of "free coloreds" on all three islands in 1835 was about 13,000.

From the start, the Danish administration had used free coloreds of all shades as bulwark against the overwhelming mass of slaves. The militia that cut down the St. Croix rebellion of 1740, as noted, was of that ilk, and thereafter service in the militia became a kind of "Upward Bound" program. A complex classification system, almost like the castes of the Hindus, was established and eventually brought the "free coloreds," depending on achievement and ancestry, into various strata of white society. At the very top of the social ladder were the few coloreds who were top-ranking officers in the militia; they eventually became the peers of the white upper class and could expect to be invited to Government House or to the ruling elite's dinners, teas, and other social functions, where Danish functionaries and British and Dutch merchants were not welcome. The very light-skinned, if they travelled, were accorded the honorifics of "Mr." or "Mrs." on their passports, and some were granted "burghers' briefs" (merchants' licenses), enabling them to become businessmen, landowners, and slaveowners. (The descendants of these people today are the Cabots, Lees, and Vanderbilts of the Virgin Islands.) Lower-grade officers of the militia and some important colored civilians occupied the second rank of the caste system, and noncommissioned officers and privates the third. With such groups of part Negro blood accepted as equals by most whites of similar social and economic status, there was established early in the Virgins an ease and accommodation between the races—so long as those of African descent were free—that remained unbroken until the early days of American ownership. Even those free coloreds not included in the Danish caste system had a position much above that of freedmen in the United States. Many moved into government jobs (thus establishing the undue desirability of having such status, which everybody in the Virgins today seems to lust after). All of the free coloreds exhibited their special position by their dress. At first it was marked only by a silver cockade, but later by the wearing of full formal European garb. (To this day there is a great formality of attire in the Virgin Islands. Despite the hot and humid climate, few adult native males appear at an after-dark affair without a coat and tie, even though both may be quickly shed, and few women without stockings and white gloves. The forms of respectability, stemming from the old Danish days, are deeply ingrained.)

While the free coloreds on St. Thomas were making progress, the condition of the blacks on St. Croix remained about the same as that of slaves in Mississippi. In 1835, more than

22,000 of the island's population of about 26,000 were slaves of the lowest form, field hands, living in a world of labor that began at sunup and ended at sundown, a world of "obeah" and "jumbis" (voodoo and evil spirits), of oppression and the constant threat of arbitrary punishment. But they were also living in a Caribbean colonialism through which the winds of change were blowing. Starting in the mid-nineteenth century, the government in Copenhagen had issued orders that the slaves were to be treated with a degree of humanity, and the dire punishments of earlier years were softened. Moravian missionaries, whose yellow-washed churches with high-peaked roofs still dot the islands, had brought education and the thin solace of Christianity to some of the slaves. And enlightened people everywhere in Europe and the Western Hemisphere were beginning to sense the enormity of the crime against humanity that slavery was.

In 1827, King Frederick VI appointed a new governor for the islands, a man who was to become a combination John Brown and Abraham Lincoln for the bound blacks. He was Peter von Scholten, an army officer with long colonial experience who had gone to the Virgins in 1804 as an ensign, the most junior of officers, and later became one of the king's military aides. As a young officer, von Scholten had learned the Creole dialect of the slaves and had moved freely among them. Once installed in Government House, he carried this familiarity even further; he installed as his hostess and bedmate the beautiful daughter of a freed slave, whom he kept with him for the rest of his life but could not make his wife because of the laws against marital miscegination. This domestic arrangement upset the conservative planters' society, which was even more upset when von Scholten began urging the king to institute procedures that would eventually lead to freedom for all the slaves. After the successful campaign in England of Wilberforce and Clarkson that in 1833 ended slavery in the British West Indies, von Scholten's pleas to Copenhagen, backed up by frequent trips home to argue the case, became more urgent. In 1847, a program of "gradualism" was adopted. Children born of slaves in the succeeding twelve years were to be free at birth and, at the end of twelve years, all slaves were to be free.

Unfortunately, this gradualism worked no better than a similar approach to ensure civil rights in the Southern states worked after the U.S. Supreme Court's 1954 decision on school integration. To the beat of drums, the ringing of bells, and the honk of conch shells, St. Croix's slaves rose on July 3, 1848, and marched on Frederiksted, where von Scholten happened to be. They numbered more than eight thousand, many more than the entire white population of the whole island, and were led by a young slave named Bhuddoe, a friend of the governor. Massed outside Frederiksted fort, the slaves threatened to burn the fort and the plantations if they were not given "freedom now."

Von Scholten acted immediately. "Now you are all free," he shouted down from the walls of the fort. "You are emancipated."

This on-the-spot decision stuck, even though the governor, under pressure from the planters, subsequently resigned and went home to be tried for dereliction of duty—a charge finally thrown out by Denmark's Supreme Court. The slaves of the Virgin Islands, fifteen years before Lincoln's Emancipation Proclamation, had become their own masters.

The new freedom, as in the American South after the Civil War, was less than absolute. The colonial council passed ordinances requiring former slaves, in effect, to become sharecroppers tied to the plantations on year-long contracts. As the years passed, the sugar business suffered a severe decline from the competition of beet sugar—a much more severe decline in the Virgins than elsewhere in the West Indies, where growing conditions were better. By 1851, sugar planting on St. Thomas and St. John virtually ceased, and St. Croix acreage had decreased nearly one third from its turn-of-the-century peak by the same year. Dire poverty became the lot of the freed slaves—poverty that resulted in labor riots on St. Croix in 1878 in which most of Frederiksted was burned and dozens of plantation "greathouses" and many sugar factories were destroyed.

*   *   *

Even before the riots, the Virgins were in serious trouble—enough to prompt discussion in the Danish Parliament as early as 1852 about the possibility of selling the place. National pride won over economics and talk of the sale stopped, but it revived again after Denmark's loss of Schleswig and Holstein in its 1864 war with Prussia and Austria. The American Minister in Copenhagen suggested to Abraham Lincoln's Secretary of State, William H. Seward, that the United States should investigate the possibility of buying the islands, if for no other reason than to pre-empt their sale to a European nation. There was at the time another compelling reason for the Union to consider the purchase. Its navy, with no base of operations in Southern waters, was having a difficult time coping with the fast Confederate blockade runners, which used the West Indies as a lurking place before sneaking into ports with their much-needed cargoes. Seward broached the subject of negotiations with President Lincoln, who gave his approval.

But the moment for the United States to take over the Virgins had not yet arrived. Lincoln's assassination and the serious wounding of Seward that occurred the same night delayed negotiations. Haggling over price followed. A treaty finally was signed October 24, 1867, agreeing to the sale of St. Thomas and St. John (the sale of St. Croix was restricted by Denmark's eighteenth-century treaty arrangements with France) for $7.5 million, a half million more than Seward had paid for Alaska. The treaty was approved by the Danish Parliament and a plebescite was held among the qualified voters of the Virgins. The transfer was overwhelmingly affirmed, with the people of St. John voting unanimously to become a part of the United States. Nevertheless, the deal fell through. Domestic American politics stood in the way. The Chairman of the Senate Foreign Relations Committee, Charles Sumner, who hated Seward and was implacable in his opposition to President Andrew Johnson, had the treaty shelved. It remained shelved until April 14, 1870, the end of the waiting period for ratification, when it expired.

American interest in the purchase of the islands did not die. In 1873, there were rumors that Denmark was about to hand over the Virgins to Germany for the return of Schleswig. Ulysses S. Grant's Secretary of State, Hamilton Fish, approached the Germans about the matter but was told that they "would not even accept the islands as a gift." Private American operators with Danish connections entered the picture in the 1890s, lured by the possibility of keeping 10 per cent of the sale price as a commission, but their *sub rosa* dealings were interrupted by the Spanish-American War. When negotiations resumed in 1900, a Standard Oil vice-president joined the group. He boasted that he had "26 senators in his pocket" and could deliver a treaty for the price of a Standard depot on St. Thomas. There were additional forces at work. The Republican Party had had a taste of empire. It was possession-hungry and in this lust was supported by navy's geopolitical publicist Rear Admiral Alfred Thayer Mahan, who called ownership of the Virgins vital to the United States. Moreover, rumors of European (especially German) interest in the place kept whetting the appetites of the new-born American imperialists.

Binational negotiations were begun again (the private operators having been shut out), and this time the Danes lowered their selling price to $5 million. The U.S. Senate quickly ratified a treaty of purchase. But although the lower house of the Danish Parliament approved the sale, in the upper house—some say because of pro-German influence among its aristocratic members—the vote was tied, nullifying the transaction. By now, economic conditions were so bad in the Virgins that two Danish government investigating commissions were sent out to see what could be done. Their findings were depressing.

During the years after the St. Croix labor riots, a large proportion of the planters had given up and gone back to Europe—to Denmark, or to other countries from which their ancestors had come. Some had divided their land among their former slaves (those blacks who hung onto their holdings were to make pots of money in the 1960s), while others had merely walked away from their lands and houses, leaving them to be over-run by the fast tropical growth. Sabra Holbrook in *The American West Indies* describes the period between 1878 and World War I:

> Although the government of the islands remained Danish, the people of the islands were left pretty much alone. They raised pigs, chickens, goats, and some cattle. They grew vegetables. They fished. When the sea receded from inland ponds, they took the salt it left. They burned charcoal for cooking fuel, as they had always done. . . . If storm or drought destroyed what they had, they began over again, perhaps on another hillside.

By 1916, the islands were $3.75 million in arrears on debts owed to Copenhagen and were operating at a net loss of $190,000 annually. The Danish government's second commission estimated that it would cost $2,240,000—in pre-World War I money—just to take care of the islands' most pressing needs. (An idea of how tough things were can be formed by considering that a dynamic black labor leader, D. Hamilton Jackson, in 1916 got field hands' wages increased from twenty-five cents a day to thirty-five cents a day and the price paid laborers at St. Thomas's ship-coaling station upped from one cent to two cents per basket carried.) Some Danish funds were forthcoming. Dock improvements were made, a drydock company financed, schools improved, and a lottery (still in existence) established to raise revenue.

When the United States finally did purchase the Virgin Islands, it was done in a state of near-panic. The Kaiser's armies had swept through Belgium, had been halted almost at the gates of Paris, had shattered the Russian armies at Tannenburg, and seemed capable of taking over Europe, including Denmark. American naval strategists feared that, in the latter event, the Germans would also take over the Virgins and effectively neutralize the approaches to the United States' Panama Canal. The Wilson administration began urgent negotiations with Copenhagen. Knowing they were in the driver's seat, the Danes upped the price to $25 million, five times as much as they had asked only fourteen years before. The United States was in no mood to bargain, and on April 4, 1916, Secretary of State Robert Lansing and the Danish Minister to the United States, Constantin Brun, signed a treaty in New York's Biltmore Hotel turning over St. Thomas, St. John, and St. Croix to the United States. Formalities of ratification moved slowly. Nearly a year elapsed before Lansing handed over to the Danish representative in Washington a draft for $25 million, an amount that worked out to $290 an acre, making the islands the most expensive piece of real estate ever bought by the U.S. government outside its own boundaries.

Money in hand, the Danes transferred the Virgins to their new overlords, the U.S. Navy.

3. Poorhouse of the Caribbean

The band of musicians selected to play the U.S. National Anthem as the Stars and Stripes was raised for the first time over the Virgin Islands on March 31, 1917, could not have been a more fitting choice for the occasion. They came off the U.S.S. *Olympia,* which had been Commodore George Dewey's flagship at the Battle of Manila Bay, where, with the destruction of a feckless Spanish fleet, the United States began its first overseas colonial adventure. Now the country was off on another such adventure, as ill-prepared as it had been for Aguinaldo and the Moros in the faraway Philippines.

For the Danes, the occasion marked the end of 245 years and 6 days of unprofitable colonialism. It is unlikely that there were many tears shed as Captain Hans Konow, last of a line of forty-nine royal and company governors, led his gendarmerie and an honor guard of sailors from the cruiser *Valkyrien* in a last parade to the sea front to begin the voyage home. In the safe of the Danish legation in Washington was a warrant for $25 million "in gold coin of the United States," a cozy bailout from a very bad situation.

The *Valkyrien,* which had been stationed in St. Thomas harbor for more than two years to overawe restive black laborers, took back with her to Copenhagen not only Danish officialdom but also, under the treaty of purchase—which gave the Danes valuable economic concessions and the rights to all "movables"—the furniture, hangings, silver, and, if reports are to be believed, even some of the wallpaper from Government House and the rope from its flagpole.*

It was not a good time for a new American venture. Two days after the Danes pulled out, the first session of the Seventy-fourth Congress convened in Washington to hear President Woodrow Wilson proclaim that "the world must be made safe for democracy." Four days later—on April 6— the president signed the declaration of war against Germany. It is likely that the first navy governor, Rear Admiral James Harrison Oliver, hankered after sea command and the chance of glory and honor that war brings to professional officers, but he put ambition aside and dug dutifully into the problems of his new job. What he learned was depressing.

Four months after taking over, Admiral Oliver wrote to Secretary of the Navy Josephus Daniels listing some of his findings:

> The death rate is very high, infant mortality being particularly disgraceful to a civilized community. . . . Sanitation is in imperative need of improvement. . . . There are only about four miles of roads in St. Thomas. . . . There are practically no food crops except for a small quantity of yams and sweet potatoes. . . . The natives should be given instruction above all else in the use of their hands. . . . Social conditions are extremely bad; there is no proper family life.

The Admiral, who apparently had not heard that Secretary of State Lansing before the purchase had made optimistic estimates of the Virgins' financial potential, bluntly told Secretary Daniels, "The islands are incapable of self-support"

---

* Just after World War I, an American journalist jokingly suggested to a Danish resident that the bust of King Frederick VI, during whose reign the slaves were freed, be removed from Emancipation Garden and replaced with one of President Lincoln. "Ach, no," said the Dane heatedly. "You can't do that. It's in the treaty."

and recommended spending nearly $2 million—an astronomical figure in those days—to put them in shape. "This unfortunate situation," he said, "is the natural, inevitable result of centuries of neglect."

The navy set about attacking the problems of the Virgins with all the zeal its destroyers were showing in eliminating the German U-boat menace in the North Atlantic. But administering the West Indian islands was even more difficult than wresting control of those dark and tumultuous waters; Admiral Oliver's command found itself in a Sargasso Sea of civil problems where propellors frequently became fouled. He chose as his first targets public health and education. It would be hard to fault him for his decision. More than forty years later, American aid technicians in "underdeveloped countries" would see such programs as a panacea for the problems of economic growth—and would find their results as disappointing as those of Admiral Oliver.

There is no question that the health of the residents of the Virgin Islands was in need of improvement. Between 1911 and 1917, nearly a third of the infants born each year died before their first birthday—320 per 1,000 live births, about three times the rate, itself deplorable, then prevailing in the continental United States. The debilitating disease of malaria was endemic. Gastroenteritis, which can be a camouflage word for cholera, was a frequent killer. Also prevalent were "big leg" (elephantiasis, caused by filaria-bearing mosquitoes), diptheria, leprosy, typhoid, and most of the other ills that man is heir to. There was no public water supply worthy of the name, few wells, and virtually no springs. Water for drinking, washing, and commercial use came from the sky and was caught in small catchment basins, rooftops, and behind crude dams. It was then piped to cisterns into which it was deposited along with all the unsavory things it had carried along.

Sanitation measures were no better than they had been in

the days of George Iversen, the Danish West India Company's first governor. The people of the towns—Charlotte Amalie, Frederiksted, and Christiansted—a majority of the islands' population, depended on the ancient and noisome convenience of night-soil removal, with women laborers carrying buckets of the stuff on their heads down to the sea before dawn each morning. (As late as the middle 1960s, a third of urban sewage on all three islands was still disposed of in this manner.) Admiral Oliver was especially distressed by the discharge of sewage into Charlotte Amalie Harbor, noting in a report to the secretary of the navy that the ebb and flow of the tide was only eighteen inches and recommending that some other system of sanitation should be devised. (The tidal flow has not changed in the ensuing fifty-five years. But the amount of effluent pouring into the harbor has increased.)

The islands' educational system was primitive in the extreme. There were nineteen elementary schools and no high schools. Most of the teachers, whose average pay was $18 a month, had no more than an elementary education, and the total school budget was $21,500 a year—less than $1 per capita. The whites and the better-off colored sent their children "off island" to school or to the few private and parochial schools available on the Virgins.

The navy approached these and other problems as a ship's captain might approach the problem of a recalcitrant crew. And it was a recalcitrant crew, with plenty of sea lawyers among its members. There were many obstacles to be overcome before the Virgins could become a taut ship.

The treaty of purchase called for retention of the Danish governmental system and basic laws until the U.S. Congress should take action otherwise, and also protected the Danish-owned companies that controlled the harbor of Charlotte Amalie, the telephone system, electric power, telegraph cables, and even the issuance of currency. (The Danish-owned

West Indian Bank had a monopoly on banknotes that continued until 1934.) With a war in Europe to fight, Congress paid little attention to the domestic affairs of the islands. It allowed the Danish governmental system to remain in force, which limited the vote to males above the age of twenty-five who had lived on the islands for five years and had an income of more than $300 a year. Although $300 was not much even in 1917, there were only 700 eligible voters out of a population of 26,000. St. Croix and St. Thomas-St. John (the latter two have always been lumped together for administrative purposes) each had its own colonial council, and each council ran its bailiwick as if the other did not exist. The taxing systems were different, local ordinances were different, administrative staffing was different, and the economies were different. St. Croix was a sugar island, dominated by the Danish-owned West Indies Sugar Factory, Ltd., which held 13,000 acres of land, employed 1,000 workers, and ran the place. St. Thomas was dominated by traders, merchants, and bankers. (St. John, whose residents had declined to 900, didn't count for much one way or another.) One navy governor was to observe, "It's like running two different countries."

The navy brought great energy and imagination to its tasks, but it also brought to the islands a vicious product that the Virgins, for all their troubles, had not really known before: racial prejudice of the truly mindless sort that existed in the United States. There had been discrimination in the Danish West Indies before the navy sailed in, but it had been based on class and caste distinctions rather than outright racism, which made any man with any black ancestry lower than the lowest white. Between the black field hands at the bottom and the establishment whites, coloreds, and blacks who had made it at the top there were permutations beyond the ken of the naval officers in charge of government operations, and especially incomprehensible to the enlisted men and Marines they had brought with them. To most of the navy, it was a strange world into which they had been transported, where, under old Danish social habits, men of color moved in the highest circles and were even invited to Government House, while whites of lower station could only envy them. Also, a sizable portion of the officers of the 1917 navy—as of all the military services—was from the South. The social attitudes and ingrained views of the Virginian or Georgian or Texan made for a very sticky situation. Then, as now, the Virgin Islander was supersensitive about being treated as a lesser breed, and his pride was severely lacerated by the newcomers' attitude. Memories of those days still rankle oldsters.

The extent of the prejudice displayed by the Southerners among the naval officers was not much worse than that of the mass of Americans of the period. It is quite unsettling in the 1970s to confront the white supremacy automatically displayed by writers for the topical magazines of fifty years ago who flocked to the islands to do stories about "our Caribbean Gibraltar," as the *National Geographic Magazine* enthusiastically called the nation's new possession. Donald Henderson, writing in the December, 1919, issue of *McClure's,* exemplified this attitude: "The Negro element is largely composed of men of untrained and primitive minds." Harry A. Franck, peripatetic ace for *Century Magazine,* went further. In the September, 1920, issue he wrote, "The loose-kneed stroll of the Virgin Islander is typical of all his processes, mental, moral, or physical."

Franck had a lot of fun writing about the islands. "The admiral-governor," he said, "gave a reception to the natives. Food was provided for five hundred and was carried off by the first hundred street women and urchins who surged through the door. The next day a large crowd came to demand their share, saying they had got nothing the day before." He concluded his piece by quoting a black woman who was sitting at the foot of one of the precipitous climbs that separate one part of Charlotte Amalie from another: "Me knees jes wilfully refuse to carry me up dem steps." Then Franck sternly observed, "That is the trouble with most Virgin Islanders. Their own knees jes wilfully refuse to carry them up the stairway to civilization. They will have to be lifted or boosted."

Not until after the doughboys came home from World War I did Congress pay any real attention to the Virgin Islands. It did so then largely because the colonial possession was costing money. Appropriations had been running more than a quarter of a million dollars annually since 1917, and the additional expense of maintaining the naval government was about $300,000 a year. The islanders' own contribution to governmental upkeep was slightly less than the federal appropriation—and considerably less than it had been in days of the Danish occupation, in the nineteenth century. A joint Senate-House commission made an inspection tour of the Virgins in the late winter months of 1920 (a visiting period favored by congressmen to this day) and came back shocked by what they had found. The shock had little to do with the efficiency of the naval administration. It had been caused by the free and easy way the United States' new wards in the Caribbean comported themselves.

"The morals of these islands are at a very low ebb," the commission report said. "Indeed, the amount of immorality is rather appalling."

What shook up the moralistic congressmen was the number of bastards. They had learned that 60 per cent of the children born each year in the Virgin Islands were the off-spring of unwed parents. It should not have required a trip to discover this, for the Bureau of the Census in 1917, after doing a special counting, had already published the figures. The cool eyes of the statisticians had discovered something else that apparently escaped the notice of the visiting congressmen. True, the number of illegitimate births was shockingly high, but the vast majority of them were to parents living together as man and wife, albeit informally. The Bureau of the Census, which is clinical in its approach to facts, had had to devise a new category for these people. It called them "consentually married." The ratio of those consentually married to those legally joined was about three to four—and the Census report said that this ratio probably was in error because many of those questioned "did not answer the questions honestly." (In this 1917 report, the Census ascribed the large proportion of "consentually married" to the high cost of the legal or church ceremony, "a strong force of custom which has existed for many generations," and "the absence, especially among Negroes and mixed, of strong public sentiment against such unions.")

The congressmen's offended reaction to the marital and sexual practices they discovered brought no sudden change in the islanders' mores. The naval governor's report for 1926 listed illegitimate births for all three islands at 59.2 per cent. On St. Croix, 67 per cent of all babies were born out of wedlock, apparently despite the fact, as the governor rather plaintively noted, that "the people are very religious and like to attend church," and the further fact that he had cut the cost of a civil marriage ceremony to $1.40. The bargain failed to attract many takers.

Not only did the navy have little success in coping with cohabitation. It made only small headway in improving the general lot of Virgin Islanders. Economic conditions stagnated. Badly hurt by Prohibition, which closed the rum distilleries, and by the falling off of shipping and the use of St. Thomas as an *entrepôt* for West Indian distribution and trade, residents left the islands by the thousands. The population dropped nearly 15 per cent during the first decade of navy rule. Fair progress was made in improving health conditions, and some roads were built and others improved.

A reasonably good water system was installed, involving the construction of large paved catchment areas on the steep hillsides to collect rainwater for storage in protected tanks and reservoirs. But most of the actions taken by the navy were at best half-hearted. Although Admiral Oliver, in his first report to the secretary of the navy, cited the urgent need for local food production, little was done to encourage it. In fact, for a lengthy period after 1924, the head of the islands' agriculture department was the base chaplain. This lay pursuit was, in service parlance, "in addition to other duties." The chaplain, according to Luther Evans in *The Virgin Islands: From Naval Base to New Deal,* "well recognized his limitations for the new task and repeatedly recommended in his annual reports that they be entrusted to an agricultural expert," but this was never done. In fact, the chaplain was given the additional duties of the welfare department.

This small criticism of navy rule was about as far as Evans, a bureaucrat's bureaucrat, allowed himself to go. But a small group of other observers looked at the navy's performance differently. Arthur Warner, associate editor of the *Nation,* after a lengthy visit to the islands in 1923, had described what the navy was doing as "a combination of archaic monarchism and modern militarism." Just as the U.S. military enjoyed extraterritorial privileges in so many places around the world after World War II, sailors and Marines stationed in the Virgins, even though it was a U.S. Territory, were outside Virgin Islands jurisdiction and could not be arrested by the local police—who, of course, were overwhelmingly black. (The Virgin Islands *Daily News,* in its fortieth anniversary edition of August 1, 1970, recollected: "Naturally, the citizenry resented this virtual dictatorship, and frequently did battle in the dark of night. Oldtime residents can remember when buildings in Savan and Frenchman's Hill bore the marks of bullets fired by trigger-happy Marines.")

*   *   *

In 1929, Herbert Hoover, "the Great Engineer," assumed the U.S. presidency. Disgruntled Virgin Islands residents who had been complaining about their lot to Washington for years redoubled their cries for help. As it happened, surprisingly, they were heard. The administration promptly sent the Director of the Bureau of Efficiency, Herbert D. Brown, to the islands to make a thorough study of the situation. His bureau (which merged with the Bureau of the Budget in 1935) was responsible for overseeing the government's management procedures and techniques. Brown, who has been described as a man of extraordinary energy and self-confidence, arrived in St. Thomas accompanied by his equally overwhelming wife, who was to assist him in his investigations.

The peacetime naval establishment, whose first rule of conduct has always been "don't make waves," had difficulties from the start with the Browns as man and wife swept through offices asking questions, examining records, looking, taking notes, and generally getting under foot. The couple spent eight months on the islands, then returned to Washington where Brown wrote a long report on his findings. He set up three options for Washington:

1. Let the Virgin Islands live on their own resources as the rest of the West Indies were doing.
2. Continue appropriations as they had been in the past, with the possibility of eventual progress.
3. Increase appropriations sufficiently to do "energetically and at once the things that are necessary to bring about improved conditions," with the ultimate goal of making the islands self-supporting.

While the report was being written, the Danish company that controlled the sugar business on St. Croix, because of the industry's economic difficulties, closed out its operations overnight and went away, leaving a thousand workers without jobs and several hundred other islanders who had been dependent on the company's activities for their livelihood without a source of income. If it had not been for Red Cross emergency food supplies, it is likely that people on St. Croix would have starved to death, for during the 1930–31 period, about 25 per cent of the island's population had to rely entirely on the Red Cross for sustenance.

Long before the word "depression" entered the statesider's consciousness, the Virgins were in one. Moreover, the Depression in the Virgins soon touched depths that even the worst-hit areas of the Appalachian coal fields, the wheat belt of the Midwest, or the steel towns of Pennsylvania and Indiana never experienced. About half of the islands' work-force was without jobs from 1930 to 1933.

The Hoover administration, to its credit, was aware of the seriousness of the situation and supported Brown's rehabilitation recommendations before Congress, which came through with the necessary funds for what can only be called a "New Deal" program two years before Franklin Delano Roosevelt was even nominated for the presidency. (In acting on the Brown program, Congress ignored the angry reactions of the naval governor, Captain Waldo Evans, who thought rehabilitation "a fool scheme" full of "visionary things.") And, at the beginning of 1931, the president by executive order took control of the islands away from the navy and gave it to the Department of the Interior, then headed by his friend Dr. Frank Lyman Wilbur, former president of Stanford University. Thus, after fourteen years of benign neglect by the U.S. Navy, were the Virgins removed from military rule.

Secretary Wilbur was given the task of finding a civilian governor to administer Brown's rehabilitation program. Sensibly enough, he went to the program's deviser for suggestions. Brown after a search found just the man: A professor at Swarthmore College in suburban Philadelphia named Paul M. Pearson. Like Brown—and President Hoover himself—Pearson was a Quaker. He was also a popular public lecturer and the moving spirit behind that cultural tent show so ubiquitous in the early years of this century—the Eastern Chautauqua Circuit. Just how these diverse qualifications fitted him for the job of governing the American Virgins is not clear, but he had no trouble getting confirmed by the Senate. After issuing an ebullient statement in Washington about the improvements he hoped to make, Paul Pearson sailed for St. Thomas, where, on March 18, 1931, the U.S. Navy weighed anchor and he was sworn in as the Virgins' first civil governor.

* * *

Trouble for the new Quaker governor was not long in coming. Eight days after Pearson's inaugural ceremonies, President Hoover and Secretary Wilbur arrived on the battleship *Arizona* on an inspection tour. It was a rather unfair thing to do to an appointee who probably was still unpacking. After a day with Pearson on St. Thomas, where the first president ever to visit was greeted with the uninhibited enthusiasm Virgin Islanders can put into any kind of celebration, Hoover departed on the *Arizona* for Puerto Rico. He had looked at what he was able to see of St. Thomas with his hard engineer's eyes, and when the battleship anchored in the harbor of San Juan, he called in the reporters who were on the cruise and fired a shot that still rings in the ears of Virgin Islanders.

"The Virgin Islands," President Herbert Hoover said, "may have some military value at some time. Opinion upon this question is much divided. In any event, when we paid $25 million for them, we acquired an effective poorhouse, comprising 90 per cent of the population."

Nor did he stop with that stunner.

"The people cannot be self-supporting either in living or government without the discovery of new methods and resources. Viewed from every point except remote naval contingencies, it was unfortunate that we ever acquired these islands," he went on. "Nevertheless, having assumed responsibility, we must do our best to assist the inhabitants."

Hoover's analysis of the islands was brutally frank. It also was unfortunately accurate. Not unexpectedly, islanders of all classes, colorations, and positions reacted angrily to it, but even though the St. Thomas *Mail Notes* editorially wished that the Danes had kept the islands and labeled Hoover's statement "devoid of decency," everybody knew deep down that the president was right. However, island pride—a strong, inflexible pride that went far beyond the understanding of Washington—was badly hurt. The people were to harbor their bitterness against Hoover for a long time; it still exists today. At the moment, however, their resentment focused on Hoover's representative on the ground—their new governor, who had scarcely had time to get his first sunburn.

Fortunately, Paul Pearson was a son of the optimistic Midwest of the early twentieth century and, remember, the builder of Chautauqua, with its emphasis on the goodness of man and the importance of his cultural development and personal involvement through learning. One of the first things this undaunted bringer-of-light did was to put on a production of Gilbert and Sullivan's "Pinafore" with a native cast recruited by a Chautauqua-type he had brought with him to tone up the cultural climate. Pearson's approach was by no means restricted to tent-show antics, however. He plunged vigorously ahead with what Luther Evans's book describes as "boyish enthusiasm" to put the Brown rehabilitation recommendations into practice. Unfortunately, in so doing, he paid no attention to the advice that Brown showered upon him and so enraged the Bureau of Efficiency's chief that by April 25, Brown wrote to Secretary Wilbur saying that Governor Pearson, the man he had himself recommended for the job, was "inefficient, unexperienced in administration, dishonest, and suffering from delusions of grandeur."

During the thirty-eight days it took Brown to get up his head of steam, Pearson, as if taking a leaf from the book of his seventeenth-century Danish predecessor, John Lorentz, had been bombarding Washington with reports and messages about what he was doing. In addition, he knew the value of publicity and filled visiting stateside newspapermen with facts and figures about programs begun and progress made. The newsmen had quickly given him not only good press back home but a catchy title as well: "The Experimenting Quaker."* The result was that Brown's plaints to Secretary Wilbur were ignored; in fact, the secretary assured Pearson of his support and told him to go ahead as he saw fit.

U.S. government reports are made on a fiscal-year basis —from July 1 through July 30 of the following calendar year. Out of his first 109 days in the post of governor, Pearson was able to put together a 34-page report that listed 24 specific "accomplishments" made since he had landed on March 18. These included obtaining an option on property to build a tourist hotel, surveying the bay oil industry and fisheries, establishing four playgrounds, beginning road construction, potting 70,000 tree sprouts for reforestation, distributing seeds for home gardens, organizing cooperatives of cattlemen, basketmakers, and charcoal burners, and establishing "cottage industries" in rug making and needlework. In addition, the governor said that negotiations had been started to purchase land for homesteading, a scheme Herbert Brown had espoused earlier.

Homesteading seemed to have real possibilities for improving the general lot of the islanders. Ninety per cent of the

* Governor Pearson's dash was inherited by his son, columnist Drew Pearson, one of whose lesser-known feats was talking his way into the Versailles Peace Conference as the correspondent of the Swarthmore College newspaper, the *Phoenix*.

land was owned by 273 individuals and corporations. In balder terms, 60 per cent of St. Thomas had 15 owners, 70 per cent of St. Croix had 14 owners, and 80 per cent of St. John had 12 owners. Under old Danish law, still in effect, unused land was not taxed, so big landowners made use of their holdings only when and if it suited them to do so. Large parts of the islands were nothing but jungle and wild cane, interspersed here and there with clearings held by squatters or "renters" who paid rent when they could, which was infrequently. The Brown-Pearson homesteading scheme appeared to promise laborers of the Virgin Islands a means of making it on their own. Terms of purchase were easy: a $19 down payment on ten acres with annual payments, including taxes and interest, of $70 for a term of twenty years. The trouble was that few would-be homesteaders had $19 for the down payment or any hope of meeting the $70 annual payments. More than 80 per cent of the islands' employed population were field hands working only 100 to 120 days a year for 80 cents a day in the cultivating season and for $1 a day in the harvesting season—an income of possibly $100 a year. Nonetheless, the homesteading program had some success; the number of farms on the islands in the 1930 census was 329; in 1940, there were 828, an increase credited to homesteading.

Many of Pearson's programs were cosmetic. The trees for reforestation died in the pots; the seeds for home gardens were not used or, on germination, withered from lack of water and cultivation; the cooperatives—an assumed economic panacea popular in that period—did not produce, and plans for the industrial and agricultural school never got off the drawing board. (Even today, there is no vocational training program in the islands worthy of the name.) All the while, the Depression deepened.

Pearson's approach to the problems of the islands, directed mostly to improving the lot of the abjectly poor, did not sit well with the so-called royal families (white, colored, and black) who owned the land, ran the businesses, and had the money. (The Virgin Islands *Daily News,* in its 1970 review, said of the situation in those days, "There was no important middle class in the Thirties. There were only the well-to-do and the very poor.") With the election of Franklin Roosevelt in 1932, this elite thought it saw a chance to rid the islands of the "Experimenting Quaker," whose radical ideas of changing things for the black lower class they feared would upset the easy life they had enjoyed for so long. To combat him they formed—ironically, as history would prove— a "Roosevelt-Garner Club" to celebrate the inauguration of the Squire of Hyde Park (who was, after all, a gentleman). Among the moving spirits of the club were members of the Lithuanian-Jewish emigré Paiewonsky family, one of whom was later to be the next-to-last appointed governor of the islands. The Roosevelt-Garner group called on Washington to send them another governor. Little did they understand the temper of the new Secretary of the Interior, Harold L. Ickes, himself a reformer of the Pearson sort. Ickes knew what Pearson was trying to do and persuaded President Roosevelt to take the unusual step of keeping the Hoover-appointed governor in his job.

So it came to pass that Pearson not only stayed on for the early, innovative years of the New Deal but was given a lot more operating room, with the result that the Virgin Islands became one of the first sites of That Man in the White House's "socialistic" experimentation. While the Tennessee Valley Authority was still largely a paper organization, a grant of $1 million by the Public Works Administration (PWA) set up the not-dissimilar Virgin Islands Company (VICO) and put the U.S. government into the businesses of sugar growing and refining, rum distilling, water supply, and power production, with a work force that eventually reached about 2,000 full- and part-time employees.

This essay into public ownership, tiny though it was, ran into difficulties when the big New Deal programs began to meet opposition from Roosevelt's opponents in the Congress, the Republican-dominated press, and other wounded but bandaged conservatives who pulled themselves together after the shock of "the One Hundred Days" of unprecedented liberal progress and started campaigning against "socialism." VICO and its successor, the Virgin Islands Corporation (VICORP), were lumped in with the TVA as a target for critics of the New Deal. Elitists in the Virgins, so lately admirers of FDR, now were on the critics' side.

Unlike the Tennessee Valley Authority, VICO/VICORP was not really a good idea. The rum the company produced under the brand name "Government House" was good and it was cheap, but Americans in the early days after Repeal were rum drinkers even less than they are now, and sales did not come up to expectations.* Also, sugar raising, as the Danes had so bitterly learned, was not suited to the Virgin Islands. Because of chancy rainfall, production averaged only about ten tons per acre, while in the fortuitously wetter British West Indies it ranged from thirty to fifty tons an acre, and in Puerto Rico, only seventy miles from St. Croix, from forty to seventy tons an acre under irrigation. St. Croix's sugar-cane acreage unfortunately was not adaptable to irrigation.

Nonetheless, New Deal money kept flowing to its island venture into state-owned enterprise—a total of nearly $3.5 million by 1938. In the five-year period, net loss on operations was about $140,000, practically a profit in those Depression years. But the infusion of federal money for VICO/VICORP and an additional $1 million or more annually in WPA grants, direct relief payments, and contributions to the islands' upkeep improved the lot of the islanders only

* Franklin Delano Roosevelt himself designed the label for Government House Rum.

slightly. Things were so bad, as the *Daily News* noted, that "native islanders left for the mainland to seek their fortunes" because conditions in the Virgins "represented a super-depression." By the mid-1930s, probably ten thousand had left, most of them for New York's Harlem.

Pearson, still undismayed, remained addicted to what Luther Evans called "exuberant enthusiasm and unexampled prediction of better things to come." Moreover, he made no attempts to mollify the important people of the islands, who, because of Danish electoral practices still existing, continued to dominate the municipal councils of St. Croix and St. Thomas-St. John and the mish-mash of commissions and bureaus that supervised island affairs. His opponents lobbied endlessly in the Roosevelt years to have Pearson removed and replaced by, of all things, a Mississippian of deepest dye named Weber Wilson, who headed the islands' judiciary. The battle got into the stateside papers, and President Roosevelt, using a tactic he frequently employed to end disputes within his administration, in the summer of 1935 removed both men from their island positions and brought them back to Washington. Pearson became an official in the Federal Housing Administration, Judge Wilson head of the parole division of the Department of Justice.

Roosevelt replaced Pearson with Lawrence W. Cramer, who had been government secretary, a job analogous to lieutenant-governor of the islands. Cramer, who was to serve until 1941, had none of Pearson's imagination and dash, but he could get along with the royal families.

If the *New York Times Index* is used as a barometer, Cramer produced the kind of calm that was wanted: For the Pearson years 1931–35, the Index lists 232 citations involving the Virgin Islands; for the succeeding six years, only 61. But uneventfulness did not mean progress. The Virgin Islands Corporation limped along, its losses covered by federal funds; the islands' revenues never even came close to paying running expenses; and the amount of WPA and direct-relief funds that had to be channeled to the islands remained as high as ever. A climate of "Washington will take care of us" was being established.

As might have been expected, Pearson, during his administration, had argued stanchly for reform of the old Danish laws under which the islands operated—a condition the *Nation* had described as "political peonage." In particular, the Quaker governor wanted universal suffrage to make residents more aware of civic responsibilities. (The electorate in 1935 was about 1,000.) In the summer of 1936, Congress passed a law that at last made the Constitution of the United States operative in the Virgin Islands, at least to a substantial degree, and swept away virtually all of the old Danish laws and practices. Among other things, this law, known as the "Basic Organic Act," gave the vote to all citizens without regard to race or sex who were "able to read and write the English language." There was, however, no outpouring of voters when the first elections under universal suffrage were held in 1938. Only a few more than 2,500 went to the polls of the more than 7,000 who were eligible to register.

As Pearl Harbor abruptly terminated the New Deal in the continental United States, so did it change the course of attempted reform in the Virgin Islands. Social and economic development took a back seat to the exigencies of mounting an ocean defense against German submarines, which, for a time, were sinking more ships in the passage between Boston and South America's River Plate than could be built in the hastily expanded stateside shipyards. But, unlike the wars of the eighteenth century, World Wars I and II brought no great economic boom to the islands. A submarine base was built and airfields expanded (largely by Puerto Rican and continental labor), but the Virgins, as President Hoover had predicted, were not important to the conduct of the war in the Atlantic and Caribbean and soon after V-J Day lapsed

again into tropical doldrums. Except for the owners of bar-
rooms and bagnios, few islanders made enormous profits during the 1941–45 period. Government and privately owned
distilleries greatly increased production, and a sizable amount
went into the production of the horrible sugar alcohol-base
liquor that was about all that could be found during the war
years. (Rum exports in 1939 were 181,000 gallons; in 1945,
1.7 million gallons of alcoholic liquor were shipped.) But
VICORP continued to lose money on its operations, as its
other ventures did not blossom.

* * *

The years immediately after World War II were among
the most exciting and certainly the most innovative of modern times. New countries became independent. The imaginative and successful Marshall Plan came into being. Instead of
a postwar slump, the United States enjoyed unprecedented
prosperity. Social attitudes changed.

President Harry S Truman, one of the changers and shak-
ers, in 1946 took the daring step of appointing a Negro as
governor of the Virgins. He was William H. Hastie, dean of
the Howard University Law School in Washington, who had
been a U.S. District Judge for the Virgins from 1937 to 1939.
Despite persistent attempts by anti-Truman senators to paint
Hastie as a Communist-liner, he was approved and on May
17, 1946, took over control of Government House in Charlotte Amalie. But the first black governor did not have much
more success than his white predecessors had had in changing things in the Virgins.

Years later Hastie, then a judge of the U.S. Circuit Court
of Appeals, went to Denmark under the auspices of the Department of State. He told the Danes a story illustrative of
the problems with the Virgins that both he and they had attempted to master. He said that during his stay a change-
over from direct current to alternating current (DC to AC)

was begun and, unexplainably, met a great deal of opposition from old residents. On inquiring about the reason for this opposition, he was told by one of his friends in the black community, "Your Excellency, the people don't want any of the American current; we want to keep the old Danish current."

4. The Development Decades

       In the early years after World War II, escape to the sun, surf, and sand of southern waters was a pastime available only to the well-heeled. And among these fortunate, only a few chose the Caribbean above Florida, Bermuda, and the Bahamas. In 1950, Cuba, with its luxury hotels, night life, casinos, and opportunities for away-from-home sin, attracted only 145,000 Americans—approximately the attendance at two professional football games in 1970. That same year a piddling 15,000 mainlanders—a very large proportion of them one-day visitors off cruise ships—went to the Virgin Islands.

       That the number was so small is understandable. It was hard to get to the Virgin Islands in those days except by steamer. Plane connections, of which there were few, had to be made in Puerto Rico, which drained off prospective visitors with its own attractions. In addition, there were not many accomodations in the Virgins of the kind that tourists typically looked for. St. Thomas had a couple of hotels, one of them started with federal funds in Paul Pearson's day, and there were "places to stay" on St. Croix, then still a "sugar island." St. John, with its magnificent but largely inaccessible beaches, by now had a population of only slightly more than 700 living in second-growth jungle. In short, the Virgin

Islands of 1950 were not very much different from what they had been in Depression days, and no travel mecca.

The February, 1956, issue of *National Geographic* featured a two-page aerial photograph of Charlotte Amalie and a large part of the island of St. Thomas. The water of the harbor appears to be brilliantly blue and the hillsides rising behind the town and the crests of the hills themselves are bare of houses. Dirt roads climb the hillside and snake their way along the top. The only "new" thing observable is the sprawling Virgin Isle Hotel, finished not long before the *Geographic*'s photographer flew over the island.

To build this hotel, now (what else?) the Virgin Isle Hilton, the broad beach at Brewer's Bay, about two miles from the site, was stripped of its sand. The builder of the hotel owned the beach, didn't he?, some people argued at the time. Development, Virgin-Islands style, had begun.

Change had in fact been under way, although its effects were not yet very apparent physically, since the mid-1950s. In 1955, the number of visitors to the islands had already risen to 91,627. Over the following five years, the number of annual visitors more than doubled, reaching 204,000 by 1960. The Virgin Islands Department of Commerce and its Tourist Board took a great deal of credit for the boom, and in fact they did attract and finance a lot of froth-producing travel writers. But the bulk of the increase was due to a trio of fortuitous circumstances. The first was the growth in the 1950s of trans-Atlantic air travel, which badly hurt the passenger-liner service. When jet planes began flying to Europe in 1958, their effect on surface travel was more devastating than that of the Germans' submarine wolf packs during World War II. (The State Department's passport division estimates that two thirds of the Americans receiving passports in 1950 traveled by ship and one third by plane; by 1960, the ratio was almost exactly the reverse.) Proud liners like the *United States,* the *Bremen,* the *France,* the *Cristo-*

foro Colombo, and others, which had breasted the Atlantic's waves at speeds up to thirty knots, became slow boats in the Caribbean cruise trade. The second change was that the emergence of the "affluent society" in the 1960s brought with it a new kind of traveler, one who wanted to go to exotic places but expected the comforts of home and no nonsense about foreign languages when he got there. Why not the American Caribbean, which had lots of glamour but no problems of coping with hotel clerks and waiters who did not speak English? The third happenstance was Fidel Castro's assumption of power in Cuba in 1959 and the imposition of the Puritanism of the Left on that formerly wide-open island. The quarter of a million Americans who were visiting Cuba annually by the time of Castro's takeover began looking for other places in the sun, and the U.S. government accelerated their switch to the nearby Virgin Islands by breaking diplomatic relations with Cuba in January, 1961. By 1962, the number of tourists who visited the Virgins in a year was nearly 300,000.

A long-time resident of St. Croix, looking back on this period not quite ten years later, told me, "We just weren't ready for what was about to happen."

* * *

Other changes concurrently in progress were also to have long-range effects.

Although voting in the 1938 election, the first held after the 1936 Basic Organic Act established universal suffrage, was light, interest in politics grew rapidly. The inclination was there. A "Republican" club had been formed as early as 1924. (One of its founders says, "A Republican administration was in charge of the national government at the time. If a Democratic administration had been in power, we might have formed a Democratic club.") But since the islanders could not vote for president and had no representation in

Congress, national party affiliation was essentially meaning-
less. Political organizations developed along social lines, divided by old animosities, rivalries, and sectional differences
rather than by ideology—and in their beginnings were clubs
into which members had to be "admitted." By 1952, two
factions existed as precipitates of the process—one the Unity
Party, the other the Donkey Democrats, so called because it
adopted the national party symbol as its own. (The Unity
Party adopted a "grass roots" symbol: a mortar and pestle,
utensils found in every island kitchen.)

The two parties—"factions" is probably a better word—
fought each other hard and sometimes viciously for control
of the two municipal councils established by the 1936 Act,
but they acted in close concert to prod the government in
Washington to broaden the political rights of Virgin Islanders. The municipal-councils system was a holdover from
Danish days with one body sitting in St. Croix and the other
in St. Thomas. Although they met in joint session at least
once yearly as the territory's legislative assembly, they were
strictly local in their lawmaking. There were separate laws
for the separate jurisdictions, different tax rates and taxing
methods, separate "treasuries," and other anomalies.

Congress in 1954 revised the Basic Act and set up a uni-
cameral legislature to serve the islands as a whole. To the
islanders' displeasure, the law did not give them all they
wanted—specifically, the right to elect their own governor
and to have a nonvoting delegate in Congress. But it did
include a seeming *lagniappe* that has since turned into a bo-
nanza: The Virgin Islands were to get back from Washington federal excise taxes collected on islands' products sold on
the mainland in an amount equal to all taxes collected by
the islands themselves. This matching system was intended
to prod the territorial government into widening its own tax
resources. The only product of the Virgin Islands subject to
the excise is rum—now taxed at the rate of $10.50 a gallon—

and the taxes collected on its sale and returned to the islands were sizable even in 1955. By 1960, without any change in taxing methods, the U.S. Treasury was returning *all* of the taxes collected on the sale of exported rum. In 1970, the amount returned was a whopping $14,111,627.

The first legislative election under the new Organic Act was held in November, 1954. Neither the Unity Party nor the Donkey Democrats were able to win a majority, but the Unity Party, with the help of an independent, whom they elected senate president, managed to organize the body in January, 1956, with a majority of one. The real power of the legislature, however, was Earle C. Ottley, then 32, a very able native black who, as a newspaper publisher and labor leader, had been in the forefront of the fight for more self-government. He continued the fight in the new legislature. The principal target of Ottley and his followers was the Republican Governor, Archie A. Alexander, a black construction engineer from the Midwest, whom President Eisenhower had appointed the year before. Alexander at his confirmation hearing had promised that he would "show those people [the Virgin Islanders] had to tighten their belts" and that he would "put people to work." Darwin Creque, a local historian, in his book *The U.S. Virgins and the Eastern Caribbean,* says of Alexander that "being a trained construction engineer, he was accustomed to obtaining results from his workers by the use of four-letter words and vitriolic outbursts"—techniques that were not popular with the employees of the Virgin Islands' overblown bureaucracy. Alexander's cardinal sin was what President Hoover's had been: Hurting local pride. Senator Ottley led a protest march of members of his Virgin Islands Labor Union against Government House, where Alexander lived and had his offices, asking for the governor's removal. About six weeks after the demonstration, Alexander resigned, pleading poor health.

The next Republican governor, Walter A. Gordon, a

black California lawyer, was less abrasive than Alexander but also seemed determined, as one politician of the day observed, "to put the natives in their place." Although it took two years for the islanders to build up a head of steam this time, the explosion when it came was even louder than the one Alexander had caused. Early in 1958, more than three thousand islanders, again led by Senator Ottley and accompanied by Valdemar Hill, Sr., president of the Unity Party, marched on Government House with a petition demanding Gordon's removal. The petition also asked that "the President of the United States publicly advocate self-government for the Virgin Islands within the framework of the United States Constitution, and announce a Plan of Action to attain this objective." Governor Gordon resigned eight months later.

That few people in Washington had any inkling of the underlying dissatisfaction of American Virgin Islanders with appointed government was demonstrated by the reaction of Democrat Clair Engle, chairman of the House Interior and Insular Affairs Committee, the group that controlled legislation for the Virgins, to the anti-Gordon demonstration. Engle said, "In the event any sizable group of Virgin Islanders demands complete self-government and independence from the United States, I stand ready to introduce legislation to achieve that status." Obviously Engle, like a lot of other people then as now, was not really listening. The Eisenhower administration, however, got the message and moved to forestall further demands. To succeed Gordon, it appointed the first native Virgin Islander, albeit a white one, John D. Merwin. A Kennedy administration consultant sent to the Virgins at the beginning of 1961 described Governor Merwin as "a man with a deft, almost Jimmy Walker touch" who was involved with no faction. Merwin managed to keep the Virgins peaceful for his full term as governor.

* * *

Critics have been knocking bricks and mortar out of the walls of Camelot ever since President John F. Kennedy's assassination, but in the New Frontier's finest hours, just before and after the inauguration, there really was high idealism at the Round Table, particularly among the squires and spear carriers of the new administration. All were eager to do the best thing possible for the new president. Stewart L. Udall, in those days one of the parfait knights, chosen to be Secretary of the Interior, dispatched two Washington consultants to the Virgins to assess the situation and come up with some possibilities for appointment as governor.

On February 13, 1961, one of the consultants, Maurice Rosenblatt, sent a memorandum of his findings to Secretary Udall, beginning, "You have in your domain one of the most exciting, promising, and potentially dangerous situations imaginable." The memo continued, presciently:

> Here in microcosm are the problems which confront America on an extended scale throughout the Caribbean and throughout much of the world: the problem of the underdeveloped country, of riches alongside poverty, absentee power, and immature local leadership, of overadministration in the bureaucracy and under-administration where vital programs languish. . . . To succeed here would be a graceful feather in our cap. . . . If you can't solve the problems of the Virgin Islands, how can America cope with the Caribbean, Latin America, and the underdeveloped countries?

Rosenblatt said he was concerned about water supply, sanitation and sewage, housing, and lack of planning for the future. He was particularly troubled by the housing situation (still, in 1972, one of the islands' most serious problems) and cited existing housing projects that had been built "in contemporary Ugly American" as what the island did *not* need. "You must improve and act," he wrote, "but do not disturb and upset the basic character and feel of the place. We must remember that the islands have only two natural resources: climate and character. While the climate remains beyond man's power to corrupt, a great deal has, could and will be done to damage and destroy the tradition, character, and physical beauty of the towns." Unfortunately, later construction continued in the mold Rosenblatt protested—and much of the newest can only be called "Uglier American."

Rosenblatt had very definite ideas on what kind of man to seek as governor. Rosenblatt wrote:

> The Governor who is needed today . . . had better be a man who can think and plan and show some initiative and judgment. This is one place where being on the spot makes a big difference and it is impossible for the Secretary of Interior to spend the time in the Virgin Islands necessary to deal with the formulation and enactment of a new program. The Governor must, therefore, be a man who will be your alter ego, sensitive to your broad policies and values, but capable of moving in the spirit of the Kennedy Administration on his own, without prompting and prodding.

Rosenblatt's memorandum examined the qualifications of four possible appointees: Dr. Alonzo G. Moron, former president of Hampton Institute, and a native of mixed blood whose white ancestors were Sephardic Jews; Dr. Aubrey Anduze, a dentist, of ancestry similar to Dr. Moron's; Ralph Paiewonsky, a rich, native-white businessman, an organizer of the Roosevelt-Garner Club, and a Democratic National Committeeman; and Connie B. Gay, the wealthy radio entrepreneur who had fallen in love with the Virgins in the early 1940s and become a legal resident, the only continental in the group.

The consultant's analysis noted rather briefly that Dr. Moron, who later attained high position in Puerto Rico, had spent less than four years of the preceding thirty on his native Virgin Islands, eliminated Dr. Anduze for similar reasons, and devoted two single-spaced pages of worried discussion to Paiewonsky, whose father, Isaac, a Jewish immigrant from

Lithuania, had come to the Virgins in 1904 as a peddler, became a merchant and the owner of a pharmacy, bought property, and when Repeal came along owned a rum distillery. Ralph became the manager of the distillery after he graduated from New York University. He also got involved in mainland politics as a member of the Democratic National Committee and as one of the two Virgin Islands delegates sent to the Democratic national conventions every four years. "With Paiewonsky as Governor," the memo concluded, "the Virgin Islands would once again become a happy pirate kingdom rivaling the days of Sir Henry Morgan, Bluebeard, and Blackbeard." Only Gay, Rosenblatt wrote, had "the capacity and drive for a task of major national importance and trust."

Gay was approached by people in the Virgin Islands to seek the job as governor. He says now that at first he did not want it, but "the idea sort of got to me." He also says that Secretary Udall did not want Paiewonsky, despite his Democratic National Committee connections, to get the appointment. Gay had the support of his fellow North Carolinians Luther Hodges, Kennedy's Secretary of Commerce, and Representative Harold Cooley, the powerful chairman of the House Agricultural Committee, both of whom urged him to accept. But the appointment did not materialize.

"I was told I was in," he reminisced to me in the course of an extensive interview at his McLean, Virginia, home. (The decorations in the front hall included an interesting exhibit that place him high in the real Washington power hierarchy: On one wall, his invitation to and the printed menu and program from one of the last dinners given in the White House by the Kennedys before JFK was assassinated; on the other, his invitation, menu, and program from the first dinner given by the Johnsons after the official period of mourning for the late President Kennedy ended.)

"On Friday I was called to the White House. You know the White House—it's a place with a lot of important people and a lot of pipsqueaks: Little pipsqueaks, middle pipsqueaks, and high pipsqueaks. One of the middle pipsqueaks took me around introducing me to everybody as 'The next governor of the Virgin Islands.' On Saturday, the next day, I called the White House and couldn't even get past the switchboard. It wasn't even 'Don't call me, I'll call you.' I just couldn't get anybody. Anyway, some time in the next week one of the little pipsqueaks called me and said I wasn't going to be governor because Papa wanted Ralph Paiewonsky. And that's what happened."

Gay did not have to identify "Papa": It was common gossip in interested circles in Washington that Joseph F. Kennedy had intervened in the selection of the islands' governor. But Gay nonetheless described "Joe's connections with Ralph's father" over the years in the liquor business, "like trading off the sale of a shipload of Virgin Islands rum for the supply of a shipload of White Horse Scotch when Joe needed it." Other sources in the Virgin Islands and elsewhere have also said that Ralph Paiewonsky's father, Isaac, played a role in Joe Kennedy's building up of a huge supply of Scotch whisky just before and after the repeal of Prohibition, a coup that helped to build the Kennedy fortune.

The appointment of Ralph M. Paiewonsky to be governor of the Virgin Islands was one of the few the Kennedy administration had difficulty getting confirmed by the Senate. Much of the opposition was based on the operation of the Paiewonsky-owned A. H. Riise distillery, of which the appointee was by then president. Witnesses told the Senate Interior and Insular Affairs Committee that Paiewonsky had obtained subsidies from the Virgin Islands legislature to pay part of the cost of molasses for rum-making, purchased from Puerto Rico, and that the Virgin Islands government had built storage tanks for him. A rival distiller, A. M. Brauer, charged that during World War II, when liquor was very scarce, Paiewonsky had evaded $1 million in tariffs by importing rum from Cuba under the Virgin Islands 6 per cent duty, labeling it Virgin Islands rum, and shipping it to the mainland. Paiewonsky indignantly denied any wrongdoing. With his attorney, Harold Leventhal, then general counsel of the Democratic National Committee, at his side, he told quizzing Senators that he had imported 5,000 barrels of Cuban rum, but "solely and exclusively for sale in the local market," and that none had been shipped to the United States. Brauer pointed out that 5,000 barrels of rum "make up to 175,000 cases"—which figures out at 2,090,000 bottles, or more than 60 bottles for every man, woman, and child then living on the islands. The Senate committee listened to the accusations but confirmed the appointment.

Paiewonsky was sworn in as governor on April 5, 1961. Secretary Udall sent one of his assistant secretaries, John A. Carver, to speak at the inauguration. The day proved a turning point for the American Virgins.

Assistant Secretary Carver brought with him a speech that, in sum, gave the Virgin Islands and their new governor a green light to go their own way unreined. Obviously, the cautionary Rosenblatt memorandum of less than two months before had been put into a dead file at the Department of the Interior.

Assistant Secretary Carver said:

> We must look to local people and their leaders to identify their problems and make known their hopes and aspirations. To the extent that these cannot be achieved by purely local effort and to the extent that they are properly a matter for federal participation, then we recognize the obligation to assume a portion of the partnership burden, just as we do in West Virginia, Illinois, or Idaho. . . . Let me say that it is not the intention of the Department of Interior to impose "administration." . . . The Organic Act conveys governmental powers to the Governor and the Legislature, and under the framework of that Act they are endowed with special accountability to

laws, not to men who may administer bureaus and departments.

The words sound good—and were doubtless well intentioned. Over the years, there certainly had been too much "administration" from men in Washington. According to an official who served in Interior's Office of Territories, "There were always twenty or twenty-five people in the Department who thought they knew more about running the Virgin Islands than the governor." But whether the abrupt and, at bottom, irresponsible separation Carver proclaimed would help to make the territory "a graceful feather" in the New Frontier's cap was open to doubt from the start—and, as it turned out, to quote another former federal official, was soon plainly recognized as "an abysmal mistake." Nevertheless, the Department of the Interior kept its word throughout the Kennedy administration and that of President Johnson as well. Today, despite obviously mounting troubles, and despite its extant, if somewhat anomalous, jurisdictional obligations, Interior continues to look on its role in the Virgins as "advisory."

Paiewonsky took over as governor at a time when the Virgin Islands still had serious economic problems, but luck and circumstances were on his side. The tourist boom that had been developing during the 1950s grew at a phenomenal rate, with an accompanying rapid increase in government revenues. Paiewonsky's inaugural speech pledged heavy emphasis on building the tourist trade, but promotion was unnecessary, for visitors flocked to the islands, willy-nilly, in ever-increasing numbers. Before the governor completed his first term in office, the numbers of visitors had increased to more than 600,000 a year and their spending to more than $54 million.

Governor Paiewonsky in his inaugural speech also promised to bring industry to the islands to take the place of the floundering sugar business, then conducted only on St. Croix and only with the help of VICORP, which had been losing nearly a half-million dollars a year—a deficit that Congress had told the Virgin Islands government it would no longer support. The Virgin Islands legislature had passed a law in 1954 to encourage industrial development through subsidies, a miniature version of Puerto Rico's *Fomento* legislation. But up to the time of Paiewonsky's governorship, the law had been used merely to assist small businesses, such as companies that imported foreign-made parts and assembled watch movements, which were then shipped to the mainland for completion.

According to a former member of the islands' legislature, President Kennedy told Paiewonsky that he would help him to interest Harvey Aluminium, Inc., a California corporation owned by a big contributor to the Democratic Party, in coming to the Virgins. Harvey was interested. And Harvey's proposition was big: A $25-million plant for the extraction of alumina from bauxite to be built on St. Croix and eventually to employ 400 workers. For its part, the Virgin Islands government, which by law retains customs duties and federal income taxes for its own use, was to exempt Harvey from all local taxes and from customs duties for a period of sixteen years and to return to the company 75 per cent of its federal income taxes during that period. Not long after, the Virgin Islands government sold Harvey two thousand acres of land, a large part of it former property of VICORP, by then out of the sugar business. Harvey paid $3 million for the land. Soon after purchase, it sold the VICORP sugar-mill equipment it got with the land to sugar interests in Venezuela for a reported $1 million.

Because the economy of St. Croix had always been based on agriculture and land was plentiful, the Paiewonsky administration started looking for agricultural enterprises to replace the defunct sugar operations. A large citrus-fruit

grower and a shipping company were found who became
very interested in the Virgin Islands when they learned they
would have tax advantages similar to Harvey's. The negotiations came to naught. The reason, says Chester Leedom, an
Interior Department official at the time, was that "the Florida
congressional delegation—and you should pardon my pun—
put the squeeze on Virgin Islands oranges." But in 1965,
another industry came the Virgin Islands way, reportedly
because of a suggestion by David Rockefeller, president of
the Chase Manhattan Bank, to Leon Hess, owner of the Hess
Oil Company, who was looking for a site for a new refinery.
Hess and the islands' government entered into an agreement
that, like Harvey's, gave the company freedom from local
taxes and customs duties and a 75 per cent return of income
taxes. In addition, with the Virgin Islands government's assistance, Hess obtained from Secretary Udall a quota to export 15,000 barrels of gasoline a day from the refinery to the
mainland. This concession, as will be seen later, was an important one.

But two industrial plants do not make a boom. The boom
was in tourism, which in no time flat was filling the government's coffers to overflowing. Taking advantage of this prosperity to provide jobs for the native population, Paiewonsky
began adding to the government payroll. When he took
office, about 2,700 people worked for the government. When
he was finished building the bureaucracy there were 7,100
—possibly 75 per cent of all native-born adults. A native lawyer, no friend of Paiewonsky, observed, "Ralph devised a mar-
velous antipoverty program. He turned most of the islands'
native poor into an instant middle class." Unfortunately for
the islands' development, however, the government payroll
ate up more than two thirds of all the money the government had for operating expenses, so that, despite sudden
affluence, little was left to build roads, schools, hospitals,
sewage plants, and all the other facilities so badly needed.

The absorption of the native work force by the government also contributed to the alien labor problem, which by 1970 was a very serious concern. It also meant that the conventional wisdom of the cynical continental, "The native Virgin Islander won't work," would go unchallenged; whether the natives would have filled the boom-created jobs or not is a question that remains unanswered.

The extraordinary growth in government revenues—520 per cent between 1963 and 1969—that made it possible to pad the government payroll was due to the uniquely advantageous revenue system under which the islands operate. Congressional beneficence, born of necessity in the "poorhouse" days but still in being, not only returns to the Virgin Islands all the taxes collected on rum on the mainland but, as noted above, allows them to keep all federal income tax collections and customs duties paid on foreign imports—and virtually all the goods in the luxury supermarkets are imported. In addition, of course, the various federal departments and agencies that make grants to state and local governments for health programs, education, highways, and the rest also make grants to the Virgin Islands, although the islanders pay no taxes into the U.S. Treasury whatsoever except estate taxes—and they are paid only on the death of residents not born on the Virgin Islands. The Virgin Islander does not need federal "revenue sharing"; he already has it all. Only a little more than 25 per cent of his local government's revenues comes from sources used by stateside local governments—real estate taxes, inheritance taxes, sales or gross-receipts taxes, licenses; the remainder, money that on the mainland goes into the U.S. Treasury, stays home. In the fifty states, the proportion of tax revenues from all sources—federal, state, and local—that goes to the federal government is 48 per cent, or $644 per capita. On the Virgin Islands, everything—$1,368 per capita—goes into the territorial coffers.

The eight growth years during which Ralph Paiewonsky

sat in the governor's chair and Senator Earle Ottley ran the legislature saw nearly a half-billion dollars flow into the islands' treasury. They spent it all—a goodly outlay for a place with a population approximating that of Dubuque, Iowa. Yet traveling around the islands at the end of this "development" era, on roads full of potholes, with steep, unprotected drops at the edges of crumbling shoulders—where there were shoulders—a visitor could only wonder where the money went. In the yards of schools that even from the outside were obviously inadequate, and seedy and rundown in the bargain, children played on rusty equipment—where there was equipment. Within sight of shacks that cried to be torn down and replaced with decent homes, there were more and more hotels, condominiums, and vacation houses for rich part-time residents. The stench too often freighting the trade winds made it quite plain that nothing had been done about sewage disposal except talk.

Also in this period, a million dollars a year in federal funds available to the Virgin Islands for sewage-disposal systems was lost because there was no concrete program. Additional federal funds for urban renewal were lost through similar inaction. Public recreation areas were turned into commercial building developments. Some doctors and staff in hospitals and clinics bought medicine and supplies, even soap and mops, because of bureaucratic delays in providing them. Fire equipment was so antiquated that trucks would break down while answering alarms and, on occasion, catch fire themselves because of overheating. An opposition candidate for the legislature in the 1970 election, recalling this period, said in a speech, "If the government of the Virgin Islands were a business undertaking, the board of directors would have got rid of the management long ago. If it were a domestic household, there would have been a divorce."

Partisan political oratory aside, the neglect of the necessary was scandalous. The trouble was that too many people were preoccupied with making money for themselves, their relatives, and their friends to pay much attention to the present and future needs of the islands or even to what was happening at a given moment to their beautiful Caribbean homeland. The spirit of the times is reflected in the title of an entertaining but biting novel Herman Wouk wrote about the Virgins, where he once owned a hilltop house: *Don't Stop the Carnival*. It was more than a carnival. It was an orgy of myopic moneymaking. Virgin Islanders with cash, political clout, or a combination of the two vied with mainland entrepreneurs, investors, and developers to grab up the beaches, the choice building sites, the old waterfront warehouses that could be converted into charming brick-walled luxury shops, and tracts of former U.S. government property, acquired by the Virgin Islands in the middle 1960s and then made available for sale or lease to insiders. Some natives who owned land—and the number had increased only a little since the years before World War II—made a lot of money. A few even became rich, but there were many others who were bilked by sharp operators, both continentals and natives. Land values went up like a moon-bound rocket; inaccessible mountain property worth $10 an acre at the beginning of the 1950s sold in half-acre "sites" for $25,000 to $40,000 by 1969.

A former resident of the islands said of those days, "If I were writing a book about the Virgin Islands, I would call it 'The $100 Million Mistake,' because that's how much money, which should have gone into schools, and hospitals, and roads, and social services, and in building things for the people of the islands, just disappeared. Don't ask me where it went, I don't know. But it went out of there by the suitcase-full."

During the throes of development, few barriers were put in the way of the profit-seekers. The islands had a planning board, organized in 1954, that was supposed "to prepare

comprehensive and general plans for the physical development of the islands," but the plan drawn up by the board
grossly underestimated the rapidity with which development
would occur and the accompanying needs that this development produced. A new plan was drawn up in 1964, in the
midst of helter-skelter growth, that has been described as
basically sound and sensible, but the legislature, whose members were benefiting from the boom, never approved it. The
islands also passed a zoning law, but almost anyone who
wanted to could build what he wanted where he wanted,
whatever the zoning regulations might have been. During
the period of greatest growth, from 1966 through 1969, only
91 applications for variations or exceptions from the zoning
requirements were turned down out of a total of 537 requested.

One wonders what the people who were running the Virgin Islands—and the Virgin Islands citizens themselves, for
that matter—were thinking about. The unique beauty that
was drawing a large portion of the visitors to "Our Caribbean Gems" was being fast destroyed. But money seemed
more important. One of the boasts of the Paiewonsky regime
was that it had persuaded the federal government, during
the period when President Lyndon B. Johnson was trying to
keep people from spending dollars in foreign lands, to give
American visitors to the Virgin Islands the right to bring
back to the mainland $200 worth of imported articles duty-
free, and five fifths of tax-free booze. (The limits for Americans returning from foreign countries are $100 duty exemp-
tion and one fifth of alcoholic liquor.) The basic appeal of
the islands was utterly ignored. There is scarcely a place anywhere that a motorist can stop with safety to look at the
ever changing view. On St. Thomas there are some forty-odd
beaches, only two of which are public. Daily charges at those
private beaches that are "open" range up to $5. The situa-
tion on St. Croix is not dissimilar, and the best beaches on

St. John are in a National Park. Tourist information services are poor, and the government employees who run them less than cooperative. The authors of *Fielding's Guide to the Caribbean: 1971* complained that even they got a minimum of assistance from the Tourist Board. Many continentals who once fell in love with the Virgins and chose to make the islands their permanent residence have sold their properties and moved back to the mainland. Even short-time visitors, after stumbling on the broken sidewalks and paying stateside prices for "duty-free" drinks, can frequently be overheard declaring that they have no intention of making a second visit. "Next time," said one man as he elbowed his way down Main Street in Charlotte Amalie, clutching Sparky's and A. S. Riise shopping bags of liquor and perfume, "I think we'll go down to one of those foreign islands where they haven't spoiled things yet."

The sad fact is that the tourist decades of the 1950s and 1960s were so marked by greed and lack of foresight, in Washington and in the territory itself, that only one of the three islands remains anything like a paradise. Each has developed along a different path. St. Thomas has been despoiled in one way, St. Croix in another, and St. John saved only by a kind of gentlemanly seduction that itself substitutes ethical problems for environmental ones. Let us look more closely at these three Virgins.

5. St. Thomas: Tourism and Hanky-Panky

The Virgin Islands Telephone Company's directory has 71 "white pages" listing the company's subscribers. But 211 "yellow pages" are needed to list the islands' bars, restaurants, hotels, gift shops, liquor stores, real estate firms, construction companies, swimming pool cleaners, television repairmen, yacht charterers, beauty shops, and other commercial enterprises created by the tourist boom. The vast majority of these businesses are on St. Thomas, which since the eighteenth century has been the Virgins' prime trading center.

The amount of business done in St. Thomas today is far beyond the wildest dreams of the Danish, Dutch, and British traders who grew rich on Charlotte Amalie's "free-port" status—an arrangement that was continued after the islands' purchase by the United States ("It's in the treaty"). The small import duty—a flat 6 per cent impost—plus the absence of federal excise taxes, special import concessions to American tourists, the excellent harbor, and a keen eye for trade have made Charlotte Amalie a mart extraordinary for baubles and booze.

The Virgin Islands Department of Commerce estimates

that about half of the more than $100 million annually spent by visitors goes to gift shops and liquor stores; about 80 per cent of this money is collected by the merchants on Charlotte Amalie's Main Street, with the liquor stores probably accounting for half of this retail business. Strong drink has always played an important part in the economic life of the island. Although George Iversen, the first governor, named the town he settled for the wife of his king, for years the place was known throughout the Caribbean as Taphuis, the Dutch word for tavern. The name was well deserved. The rum concoctions of that time—grog, toddy, and "blackstrap" (a combination of rum, molasses, and vinegar)—have given way to banana daiquiris, *piña coladas* (made with coconut cream), and other exotica of the blender, which the tourists imbibe in large quantities. But on-the-spot consumption of drinks is small compared to bulk sales in cardboard cartons especially designed to hold the tourists' "free" allowance of five fifths each. It takes a lot of whiskey, brandy, and liqueurs to meet the demands of the hordes of thirsty tourists. (In 1968, liquor imports to the islands totaled 24,325 *tons*. That same year, gasoline imports totaled 39,039 tons.)

Liquor sales are high throughout the year but reach astounding peaks when cruise ships are in port. Last year, more than 90 per cent of the 550-odd ships that stopped in the Virgins made St. Thomas a port-of-call. When the ships are in—and four or five frequently arrive on the same day—the counters of the liquor stores on Main Street are lined three and four deep with customers. The crowds are even deeper around the tables where sample tastes of liqueurs most people never heard of (all high-profit items) are dispensed. At the rear of the stores, assembly lines of packers fill the firms' distinctive cartons, seal them, and load them on trucks for delivery to the tourists' ships. Walls of liquor cartons pile up at dockside. Those from Sparky's are fluorescent yellow, those from A. H. Riise, owned by the Paiewonsky family, burgundy red, and Norman's are pale yellow, to identify three of the larger sellers.

One-day visitors who come from Puerto Rico by plane also swell liquor sales. Sparky's maintains a shop at the Harry S Truman Airport to catch them arriving or departing, and another store advertises that customers can save the round-trip San Juan-St. Thomas fare by buying its "five-pack."

The environment of Charlotte Amalie is pleasant and picturesque, conducive to spending on liquor and other luxuries. Many of the shops that extend for nearly a half-mile along Main Street are old warehouses built of ballast brick from sailing ships, coral, and volcanic rock, handsomely converted for their present use. Their high-arched doorways open onto the street, and cool air from high-powered air-conditioning units wafts through the entrances to the hot sidewalks, inviting passersby to enter. This stretch of street is a fantastic supermarket filled with Vuitton luggage, Orrefors and Waterford crystal, Piaget and Patek Philippe watches, Royal Crown Derby and Royal Doulton china, Hasselblad and Leica cameras, Zeiss binoculars, Braemar sweaters, Thai silks, dresses by the finest French and Italian designers, and perfumes rivaling in variety if not quite in quantity the whiskeys—all at "far below stateside prices." One shop, which advertises itself as "the world's largest perfumerie," as well it may be, has three cashiers and lines of customers like so many suburban housewives with carts of groceries waiting at the check-out counter.

But outside these shops, native St. Thomians, polite as they naturally are, aware as they have to be of their dependence on tourism, more and more often can be seen and felt to express, generally in subtle ways, their resentment at affluence running hogwild. Small wonder. Practically any day of the year, walking along Main Street's narrow sidewalks is like bucking the Christmas-shopping rush in a mainland city. On days when there are several big cruise ships in port, with three or four thousand bargain hunters ashore all avid to take advantage of their $200 "duty-free" allowance, progress along the street is even slower. On such days St. Thomians stay home or use the waterfront or Back Street, a narrow parallel thoroughfare of dingy shops and bars with no sidewalks, to get where they want to go.

Few tourists ever reach Market Square, beyond which Main Street is strictly old Virgin Islands, with broken pavements, uncollected trash and garbage, inoperative traffic lights, and the stores where the natives shop. Here the goods are the necessities of life, not its luxuries—and unfortunately for the resident Virgin Islander, the necessities they shop for are very dear. No decent statistics are available on what it costs to live in "American Paradise," but since everything used or consumed except building sand, rock, and gravel has to be imported, everything costs more than it does on the mainland. In a brochure on the islands published in 1970 by the First Pennsylvania Bank of Philadelphia, owners of the Virgin Islands National Bank, the First Pennsylvania's chief economist, Lawrence C. Murdoch, Jr., wrote, "The over-all cost of living averages at least 25 per cent more than in Philadelphia, in spite of the climate which makes warm clothing and home heating unnecessary."

For the tourist, too, if he is more than a one-day tripper, the cost of living on top of all his free-port shopping adds up to a very expensive vacation. A $100-a-day hotel bill for a couple is not unusual in the "season," and a $75 one is about the median. Considering that there is no federal excise tax on liquor and that the import duty, if any, is tiny, the prices of drinks are surprisingly high, about what they are in Washington, D.C., or Chicago. (It can be irksome to have a bartender charge you a dollar for a regular daiquiri in which he has put an ounce of rum that costs ninety cents a fifth in the supermarkets.) What's more, although St. Thomas is charming and exotic when viewed from the deck of an incoming ship or a circling airplane, the tourist once landed too often discovers that getting there may have been more than half the fun. Meals in the restaurants patronized by visitors are not only high priced but mediocre in quality. (One does not have to be a gourmet to feel disappointed when served taste-less frozen fish while looking out over the shimmering sea.) Historic sites are few and most of them poorly maintained, the roads better avoided, the recreational facilities—except for sailing and fishing—amazingly limited. Only a fraction of the one-day trippers and people off the cruise ships find that the arrangements made by their travel agents include easy access to the sea. Since less than a third of St. Thomas's ap-proximately 1,500 hotel rooms are in places beside the water, basking on what the Department of the Interior's pamphlet calls "some of the most beautiful beaches in the world" re-quires guests at most of the larger hotels to become prisoners of the infrequent bus service offered by their hosts.

Unlike many of the other Caribbean islands, St. Thomas has no long, unbroken, accessible stretches of sand; its beaches are mostly in bays and coves easily sequestered by the building of exclusive hotels and condominiums—and fences. One of the first things the "developers" did when the boom began was to grab up the beaches and turn them into restricted private property. By the mid-1960s, the only beaches worth the name that remained for public use were Magen's Bay, three miles from Charlotte Amalie by tortuous roads, and Lindbergh Bay, adjoining the busy airport. As a sop for the local people, the Virgin Islands government put up two small prefabricated swimming pools, one of them an ironic twenty yards from a harbor beach Charlotte Amalians used before the harbor got too polluted.

In the early months of 1971, agitation to open St. Thomas's beaches "for the free, unrestrained use by all the people of these islands" was started by a "Citizens Committee on Beaches" that obtained 2,500 signatures on a petition. The committee went on to stage "swim-ins" on some of the closed beaches. A contributor to the *Daily News*, which, like many small-town newspapers, still runs verse from its readers, summed up the island-born St. Thomian's feelings in what the paper described as a "calypoem in the native idiom." The calypoet, Corey Emanuel, wrote:

> Well, we ain't go'n beg
> An' we ain't go'n bawl
> Every beach in these Virgins
> Must be free for all!
> John and the public sure bound to agree
> That the beaches are ours an' got to be free!
>
> All this Ecology study and Environment
> Pollution, and Ethnic Disagreement
> Ain't meaning a thing to the common man
> If he can't even swim in his own native lan'!

The Virgin Islands legislature, prodded to action, came up with a bill that tried to please both the "free beaches" people and the owners of the comparatively scarce and superexpensive beachfront hotels and condominiums. One long-time white resident, sympathetic to the native view, said of the legislation, "All the bill did was just reaffirm that the public has a right to the beaches. It was like a congressional resolution that says, 'It is the sense of Congress that this or that should be done.' What was wanted was a bill with teeth in it that could be tested in court. They didn't get it. But I still think they will."

One or two of the more far-seeing and sensible beach owners have let down their bars and are allowing use of their facilities for a reduced fee or are simply not trying to stop people who come to their valuable strips of sand already dressed in bathing suits. The mainland developers of a new hotel complex now under construction have said that their beach will be open without charge to anyone and that they even hope to make money from the sale of food and drink under this policy.

Not only the beaches have been rendered off limits to the average resident St. Thomian and the less-than-loaded visitor. Thanks to the spiraling land values of the development decades, the "numerous misty mountain peaks" of the Department of the Interior's pamphleted list of assets are likewise financially out of bounds today. First Pennsylvania's economist Murdoch, in his report quoted earlier, noted in some awe that

> A single acre of raw mountainside was recently purchased for more than $150,000. To us, such prices are unbelievable. If, for instance, the whole island of St. Thomas were transplanted to central Pennsylvania, it probably would be considered too steep and rugged for human habitation. More than likely the State would buy the whole thing for a few dollars an acre and turn it into a preserve for wild birds. But located where it is, the Caribbean "birds" are willing to pay fortunes for perches on St. Thomas and the other U.S. Virgin Islands.

Those birds who came early to St. Thomas live in expensive simplicity in houses with sun decks and swimming pools and glorious views from the island's spine, eight hundred to fifteen hundred feet above the sea. Later comers have had to make do with houses on the steep slopes, where bulldozers clank from daybreak to dark as sites are cleared for still more building. Since the island's natural drainage system has long since been destroyed, fresh red earth from the construction sites streams down the hillsides during the frequent rains onto the lesser people below. There are some lovely houses left from the old Danish days on the lower levels, and these have been lovingly restored, but the rest of the island's dwellings, even with hibiscus and bougainvillea and scarlet flamboyant trees masking their decrepitude, have little to offer.

"Approximately 50 per cent of all families are living in substandard dwellings," the Virgin Islands Department of

Housing and Community Renewal said in a report on all three islands published in 1971. The situation on St. Thomas is worse than the norm. A survey done for the department in 1969 found that 1,120 out of 3,940 dwellings in the island's urban area should be torn down and that 1,335 needed "extensive rehabilitation"—in other words, they were salvageable only with a lot of work and money. Typically, the Virgin Islands government has done little to alleviate the situation. On Charlotte Amalie's waterfront, beyond Emancipation Garden and the scaly, 300-year-old Fort Christian, are nearly two square blocks of vacant land known as Barracks Yard. Here, where slum clearance began in February, 1963, nothing remains today but muddy rubble leveled for the parking of cars belonging to government employees; the displaced dwellers have moved into other slums. The Housing Department's latest report says that it has 2,120 applications on file—each representing about four persons—for "emergency housing." It had found places for *eighteen* families in the preceding year. The Virgin Islands Housing Authority, which controls the Ugly American apartment complexes and other rental units, at the same time had 3,516 applications in its files—roughly half of them from St. Thomians. The authority did not report how many families were given public rental housing during the year, but knowledgeable people outside the government say that the number was mighty small. Anything else was impossible. The authority controls less than 1,800 rental units. The possibility that many native Virgin Islanders on the waiting list will attain the much-sought-after goal of "getting in the housing" seems remote.

St. Thomians of the "instant middle class" seek to get "in the housing" just as much as the really poor do, for home ownership, that standard goal of the upwardly mobile everywhere, is especially difficult to achieve in the Virgins. Affordable land is scarce, and, according to the Housing Department, the Virgin Islands have the highest unit construction cost of any area under the American flag, not excluding Alaska with its special building problems. Moreover, these costs keep going up; they increased 40 per cent between 1965 and 1970. The Housing Department in the past few years has begun a program for "moderate income" residents, but the houses that have been built so far are abominations.

One representative development on St. Thomas consists of a huddle of a couple of hundred concrete boxes at a place in the interior of the island called Tutu, four miles from Charlotte Amalie by infrequent bus and crowded two-lane road. The houses are built on forty-by-fifty-foot lots on the lee side of two hills, have no sidewalks, no landscaping, no parking areas, no recreation or shopping facilities, and totally inadequate ventilation. "Livin' here," one resident said, "is like livin' in an oven, mon." Somehow, the Virgin Islands government has obtained Federal Housing Administration mortgage guarantees for this concrete-box development and for a half-dozen other projects on St. Thomas and the other islands. What has been produced is a gaggle of instant ghettos, poorly suited in design for tropical climate and all far from the urban areas where most natives work. The Housing Department is now in the process of topping its earlier mistakes by building row houses—grandly titled, in the realtor's usual idiom, "town houses"—just about the most unsuitable kind of housing for the Virgin Islands that could be imagined. One native critic of the government's housing program estimates that it will take ten years of building merely to catch up with present needs, and he probably is right. The consultants who did the slum-clearance survey estimated three years ago that 8,000 to 8,700 new units would be needed on St. Thomas alone by 1980 to meet the demands of non-visitor growth and to replace the slums. In the three years since the survey, about one tenth of the projected need has been met.

The government of the Virgin Islands has failed utterly to

protect the native St. Thomian against the despoilation of his environment and the closing off of his beaches. It has failed to provide him with a decent educational system, adequate housing, good health facilities, and other public amenities. What it has done is to see to it that the burst of prosperity has provided him with a job—a government job. Between 1962 and 1972 the government employment rolls on all three islands increased nearly 275 per cent to about 7,400. Salaries, wages, and fringe benefits for these people zoomed to $48 million a year. H. L. Ross, comptroller for the Virgin Islands and the only resident federal official who keeps an eye on the local government's operations, estimates that 11 out of every 100 residents work in the bureaucracy. (In October, 1966, by comparison, according to Ross, the number of state and local employees for all fifty states averaged only 3.7 per 100 residents.) But the presence of all these people in local government has also meant other failures.

In any bureaucracy, there is plenty of goofing off, but in the Virgin Islands it is done with Caribbean flair. A St. Thomas businessman figured out that government employees work about 185 days a year. "There are twenty-six holidays— all the ones you have on the mainland, plus Holy Thursday, Good Friday, and Easter Monday, and our own peculiar ones, like Boxing Day, Carnival, and Transfer Day. We're following Congress's lead, too, and shifting the time of a lot of holidays to make for three-day week-ends. And then there's sick-leave—that's about five weeks, depending on length of service. Everybody, practically everybody, takes all of the sick-leave. And then there's regular leave—thirty days a year. It's kind of hard to get any business done."

Generally speaking, getting business done with the islands' government is difficult and frustrating for the visitor from the mainland and the resident alike. The approach is almost Asian. Appointments are hard to get, and seldom can they be made on short notice. "Call me tomorrow," is a usual ploy, however urgent the inquiry may be. Finding the right person to handle one's problem or request can take hours and even days. Often there is no one person; a half-dozen officials may have to study even the simplest proposal before action is approved. The net result of this gross bureaucratic process is that lots of things just do not get done at all.

One of the things that did not get done very well during the big money boom of the 1960s was the collection and payment of bills. In 1971, Comptroller Ross found 226,000 outstanding bills, totaling more than $16 million, owing to the government—half of them outstanding a year or more, and about 10 per cent, totaling $1.7 million, outstanding for more than four years. The residents of the Virgin Islands, he found, owed $4.1 million in income taxes, and *95 per cent* of the accounts were delinquent. On the mainland, income tax delinquency of this nature would have resulted in tax liens against the offenders. Ross found that $3.9 million was owed for hospital services (the Health Department's total budget is about $10 million), and 85 per cent of the accounts were more than a year old. The Water and Power Authority, he found, had accounts receivable totaling $2.6 million, and 3,500 bills returned by the Post Office as undeliverable. But practically nobody had his water or electricity cut off.

In the summer of 1971, after several warnings to the commissioner of finance about money owed for telephone service, the Virgin Islands Telephone Company, owned by International Telephone and Telegraph, disconnected all of the government's telephones. The back bills were quickly paid and service was resumed. Other creditors of the Virgin Islands government cannot bring such direct pressure to bear. Comptroller Ross found that the Department of Health alone had more than $300,000 in unpaid bills more than a year old. He also reported, "In a limited canvass of suppliers of various government departments and agencies, we received reports of accounts that have been due as long as nine years." A medical professional at the St. Thomas hospital said that he has had to circumvent the official procurement procedures to ensure that he has supplies on hand when he needs them. "I used to practice on the mainland and I know the people in the business. They send me what I need and I pay for it, then I bill the authorities. It takes a little time to get my money but eventually I do get it. It's a cumbersome way to handle things, but luckily I can afford it and my department can do its job the way I think it needs to be done." This medical man is an exception, however. Most hospitals keep running out of soap, bandages, thermometers, surgical instruments, and other necessities. In the schools, matters are even worse. When the enormous influx of new students came in September, 1970, supplies of all kinds were lacking. Teachers asked children to bring old newspapers and magazines from home for use in art classes and had to keep textbooks in the classrooms so that they could be passed around among the pupils on a schedule. The Department of Education finally got the necessary books and supplies, but, to the government's embarrassment, it had to pay cash before delivery was made.

*　　*　　*

Where does the responsibility for this incredible mess lie? How, in less than ten years' time, was an uncrowded, easygoing, if rather rundown and raffish island transformed into an overcrowded, increasingly tense, still rundown place with too many luxury homes but not enough plain ones, muddy mountainsides, a polluted harbor, and a bureaucracy apparently incapable of coping with these and all the other problems dumped on it in so short a span? As to any question of so broad a scope, the answers are not easy.

Put the finger on Ralph Paiewonsky and Earle Ottley and the Democratic machine they built? Possibly. But, despite their thirst for power and their greed, their efforts were in many ways intended to do what they, who lived there and loved it, thought was best for the Virgin Islands and Virgin Islanders. As John J. Kirwan, former acting director of Interior's Office of Territories, wrote to me, "The real locus of power in the islands in those days lay in the working relationship between the Governor and the Senator Ottley faction which controlled the legislature through the continued and repeated approval of the informed voters. They tried to do what was best for the islands, sometimes made it, sometimes didn't. Is this too hard to believe?" No, it isn't. But the present state of affairs seems to testify that what was done by the politicians through nineteenth-century *laissez faire* development policies, government largesse in the form of jobs, and political shenanigans was not what was needed.

Might the feckless disregarded for the future have been brought under control at some point or another? Perhaps. But nobody was watching. Comptroller Ross did not come to the islands until late 1969. His predecessor, Peter Bove, during his ten years as comptroller seems to have been more of a bookkeeper than a growling critic.

The sorry truth is that, despite the warnings given to Secretary of the Interior Udall in 1961 by the consultants he sent to the Virgins, the New Frontier chose to ignore indications of danger in its tropic show window and instead sent Assistant Secretary Carver to Ralph Paiewonsky's inauguration to give the Virgin Islands government new freedom to go its own way without the Department of Interior looking over its shoulder. During his years in office under the Kennedy and Johnson administrations, Udall seldom leaned on the Virgin Islands government; in fact, he gave it most of the things it asked for, particularly in the days just before the Nixon administration took over, and he and Ralph Paiewonsky had to resign.

The Congress of the United States was even less exacting. Because of its advantageous financial position, made possible by federal tax largesse, the Virgin Islands government seldom requires appropriations, and during almost all of the Paiewonsky years did not have to face the nit-picking, line-by-line examination of purposes that is exacted of any governmental organization asking Congress for money. Consequently, the territorial subcommittees of the Interior and Insular committees of the Senate and House were practically the only legislative questioners the island government had to contend with. And there was little contention. Senators have bigger things to worry about than the affairs of a tiny place like the Virgin Islands, and the Senate subcommittee seems largely not to have bothered. The House subcommittee, dominated by Democrats with old-fashioned machine backgrounds, paid more attention, but generally as advocates of what was going on in the Virgin Islands rather than as responsible territorial overseers. When, in 1967, Ariel Melchior, Sr., the outspoken publisher of the Virgin Islands *Daily News,* tried to explain a long list of charges he had made against the Paiewonsky administration in a paid advertisement in the Washington *Post* asking for a congressional investigation, the then-subcommittee chairman, Hugh L. Carey, a Brooklyn organization Democrat, cut short Melchior's opening statement and without a break asked him thirty-eight largely irrelevant questions that can only be described as "adversary." Melchior, an honest, muckraking, sometimes choleric and abrasive newspaperman who has run the *Daily News* for forty-two years, said some years later, "They just didn't want to listen."

But if not many members of Congress wanted to spend a lot of time on the concerns of a place populated by fewer people than any congressional district, there were plenty who found the Virgins a nice place to visit. And visit they did, particularly during the Christmas-New Year recess. So did their relatives. All were warmly received.

"The Paiewonsky crew were experts at cuddling up to

people who mattered through their sons and daughters, and their wives and in-laws, and even their cousins and uncles and aunts," the caustic Connie B. Gay told me. "It was pretty hard for a man back in Congress or Interior or anywhere in the government to get critical of the Virgin Islands after Uncle John or Cousin Sarah had a ball on St. Thomas or someplace else on the islands."

Besides entertainment, there were honors and perquisites offered to people connected with high places. Mrs. Lyndon B. Johnson was made a trustee of the College of the Virgin Islands, founded by Governor Paiewonsky, and was the college's first commencement speaker. Mrs. Hubert H. Humphrey was made a director of Laurance Rockefeller's Caneel Bay Plantation on St. John. A housing project was named for the late Congressman Michael J. Kirwan before that irascible Ohio Democrat died. Congressman Wayne Aspinall, chairman of the House Committee on Interior and Insular Affairs, had a junior high school named for him. And a couple of Stewart Udall's children were given summer jobs on the islands during the Paiewonsky era.

In a hearing held in the Virgin Islands and in Washington during July, 1967, on a bill to provide for the election of the governor of the Virgin Islands, the tilt in the Democratic leadership toward the *status quo* was patent. Members and supporters of the incumbent Virgin Islands government were given the oily care congressmen usually extend only to their own colleagues; critics got the kind of imperative questions usually reserved for hostile witnesses.

Republican members, including Maryland's Rogers C. B. Morton, now Nixon's Secretary of the Interior, and Pennsylvania's John P. Saylor, frequently tried to probe beneath the surface, but their inquiries and the answers thereto were buried in the record. Another negative, if unavailing, voice raised in the halls of Congress at the time was that of Senator

Gordon Allott, Colorado Republican, who strongly demur-red from a report of the Senate Committee on Interior and Insular Affairs approving the elective governor bill. Senator Allott had tried unsuccessfully to get the then-Attorney General, Fred M. Vinson, Jr., to investigate some typical Virgin Islands high-jinks that had occurred during the 1966 legislative elections. The replies he received, over Vinson's signature, were masterpieces of bureaucratic obfuscation, so the Colorado senator presented his "individual views" when the committee's report was written. He said he was "deeply convinced" that the affairs of the islands were in such a state that they could not be freed of the executive branch's super-vision.

"Congress must initiate an investigation of the political af-fairs of the Virgin Islands," he said, "before such legislation as S. 450 [the elective governor bill] can be enacted. Any other course of action is precipitous and tantamount to a com-plete abandonment of our Constitutional responsibilities."

The bill nonetheless became law on August 23, 1968, and in November, 1970, the first elected governor of the Vir-gin Islands was chosen by the territory's citizens. Whether Senator Allott and the other Republican critics, then fretting under the dominance of the Johnson administration, should have been listened to about the timing of the Elective Gov-ernor Act is now academic.

It probably would be wrong to say flatly that official Wash-ington—the executive and legislative branches—abdicated its responsibility for the Virgin Islands in the 1960s. From 1936 onward, Washington—slowly and grudgingly, to be sure—had given the islands a large measure of self-government. But the Congress and the Department of the Interior, both as former colonial administrators with residual responsibilities under law that they shrugged off after 1961 and as institutions with general responsibility for broad federal programs involving all states and territories, did not look critically enough at what was going on in St. Thomas.

And what went on is hard to believe.

* * *

American lawmaking bodies at the state and local level have earned in the course of history a well-deserved reputation for hanky-panky. In this national pursuit, the twenty-eight year-old legislature of the Virgin Islands can claim peerdom with any mainland lawmaking body. Although truly reformist in its beginnings, during the islands' boom years it ran its business in such a way that few politically on the inside failed to profit from the new prosperity.

Since the days of the early Danish governors Nicholas and Adolph Esmit and Gabriel Milan, who lost his head for his pecadilloes, irregularities have marked the governing of the Virgins, and they still do. In one instance, not long ago, after the discovery of 110 instances of allegedly improper payments totaling $2 million that had been approved by government officials, the Virgin Islands legislature quickly passed a bill relieving each of the officials involved, by name, of any responsibility for the transactions. But it was during the anything-goes years, when tourism and tax incentives first brought wildly spiraling prosperity to the entrepreneurs lured to the islands by the tropic gold, and to the luckier, or greedier, or shrewder of the natives, that irregularities became a way of life. The style was set and abetted by the Virgin Islands legislature, controlled by the Paiewonsky-Ottley machine.

Lots of people on the inside seemed to make money—including not only senators but their relatives and friends and all those canny operators, native and continental, who had political influence. The really big bites came during the 1968–70 period, when the Paiewonsky-Ottley machine, having taken over the Democratic Party and seemingly worn out the opposition, held all fifteen seats in the legislature and engaged, as an opponent in the 1970 election campaign orotundly charged, in "cynical lawmaking for the benefit of the few" and the "buying and selling of privileges in the legislative chamber."

The Democratic machine's absolute control of the legislature had been effected in a dozen or so years of almost Byzantine political maneuverings that gave its leadership control of the only legal political party of significance. Ideologically, just about everybody in the Virgin Islands from the Hoover days onward was a "Democrat," but without voting ties to the mainland, since islanders could not—and still cannot—vote in federal elections. A Virgin Islands witness at a congressional hearing a few years ago told a puzzled congressman who was trying to sort out existing political factions, "But we're all Democrats." In the late 1950s and early 1960s, as noted, one faction was known as the Unity Party and the other as the Donkey Democrats, with the Unity Party from the time of organization of the legislature in 1954 holding control of that body, usually by a slim margin.

In 1963, the senators of the Unity Party, which had a majority of one, revised the islands' election code and set up a procedure for legally recognizing political parties, which gave all citizens the right to register in the party of their choice. The bill was signed into law by Governor Paiewonsky, a one-time Donkey Democrat who had joined forces with Earle Ottley. The Unity Party was dissolved, its members registered as Democrats, and in an election for the party's territorial committee won sixteen of twenty-two positions and control of the party. The discomfited and disarrayed Donkey Democrats filed a suit charging the former Unity Party leadership with conspiracy to take over their party, but lost in the federal Court of Appeals. In the 1964 election, the Donkey Democrats had to run as independents, and, although they kept their same relative strength in the legislature in the 1964 and 1966 elections, they ran out of steam. Between the 1966 and 1968 elections, the Paiewonsky-Ottley-controlled legislature enlarged the body's membership to 15 and in 1968 completely shut out the opposition.

During the five-year period after passage of the revised election law, the legislature also effectively shackled its only possible opponent in official position, Government Secretary Cyril E. King. King's job, a holdover from Danish days, in part approximated that of a lieutenant-governor, but it also involved numerous supervisory tasks in the fields of banking, insurance, and business. King, a native black who had served on the staff of Senator Hubert H. Humphrey for twelve years, fell out with Governor Paiewonsky at about the time the Donkey Democrats lost their party identity. By various legislative acts, the Ottley organization took away virtually all of King's functions, leaving him with little more than custodianship of the Virgin Islands seal. King stubbornly, some people think mulishly, held on to his job. Although nearly powerless, he had the support of the publisher of the *Daily News,* Melchior, who had made a career out of badgering Virgin Islands governors, lawmakers, and politicians from the time of his paper's founding. This support was to carry over into the brief period in 1969 when King was acting governor and into the first campaign for an elective governor in 1970. But the all-powerful legislature, despite efforts by a hobbled King and others and constant criticism from Melchior's *Daily News,* continued to make the most of the power it held. And the assets and privileges this tropical Tammany controlled were rich pickings.

Richest of all was the land. Through the beneficence of the federal government, the local government owned huge holdings on St. Thomas and St. Croix. The liquidation of the Virgin Islands Company had given it thousands of acres, and in 1968, when the large submarine base built on Charlotte Amalie's outskirts during World War II was sold to it at a ridiculously low price, the holdings grew even larger. Two weeks before the sale of the base was completed, Earle Ott-ley, then president of the senate, was given a lease, without competitive bidding, on a choice plot just off the main high-way to town. There he built a small building to house his newspaper, the *Home Journal*. (He rents the upper floor to an islands government agency for $570 a month.) Another senator, Louis B. Hestres, an accountant, was approached by clients who had inherited thirty acres of land on St. Thomas to check on the best tax-break they could obtain on the impending sale of the property. Hestres, who also was in the real estate business, found another buyer who was interested and, further, persuaded the government that it should acquire the property. Hestres then talked the heirs into selling the land to his buyers for about $300,000, and the new owners, in turn, sold it to the Virgin Islands govern-ment an hour or so later for more than $400,000. Charges of impropriety were brought against Hestres before the Virgin Islands Real Estate Board, but, although hearings were scheduled three times, none was ever held. Who got the $100,000-plus profit made by shuffling a few pieces of paper probably never will be officially known. In 1969, a senator from St. John, Theovald Moorehead, arranged for the sale by the government of a choice tract of property on his home island to a corporation owned by his family. The price, de-cided without competitive bidding, was set at the assessed valuation of the land five years earlier; land assessments in the Virgin Islands are 50 per cent of appraised value. A few days later, the corporation sold the land to the senator for $1. (For what it's worth, both Hestres and Moorehead were de-feated in 1970 when they ran for re-election.)

The money made from land during the boom years had its match in other kinds of profit. For one, the Industrial Incen-tive Program, with its subsidies and return of taxes, was of-ten stretched for favored persons. Although the normal period for subsidy grants is from ten to sixteen years, some, according to Comptroller Ross, have been extended as long as twenty-eight years. In addition, the legislature in many instances passed special laws giving extra benefits to favored companies. One blatant example of political use of the Industrial Incentive Program was the granting of a subsidy to a family corporation set up by David Puritz, a senator from the Sparky's liquor-stores clan, to build a warehouse. Only when Comptroller Ross, a year or so after the fact, raised questions about the propriety of the transaction was the subsidy revoked.

Appointed government officials got their share of the gravy. When conservationists, whose voices are seldom heeded in the islands, complained about the dredging of construction sand from Smith Bay on the north shore because it was endangering protecting reefs, it was learned that the Commissioner of Conservation of Cultural Affairs, on whose marshland the sand was being stored, had a cozy arrangement with the dredging contractor. The commissioner was to get to keep 50,000 tons of the sand, which turned his previously useless property into dry land suitable for development. The commissioner, whose department's responsibilities include protection of the island's beaches and "natural resources," still holds his job.

Possibly the most blatant use of the government treasury was made by Earle Ottley during his term as president of the senate. Besides being the top man in the legislature, he was also boss of the Virgin Islands Labor Union, numbering about 5,000 members, the co-boss of the Democratic Party, and publisher of the *Home Journal,* the second largest daily newspaper in the islands—a combination of jobs to make any politician drool. In July, 1968, he had passed a bill requiring that all of the government's legal advertising be published only in his St. Thomas paper and another paper on St. Croix in which he had an interest. Until this time, such advertising had been spread around among all the newspapers, with even the *Daily News,* harsh critic of the Paiewonsky-Ottley machine, and the largest paper, getting a share. Ottley set a price of $8 a column inch for the advertising, although the highest advertising rate the paper then charged was $3.50 an inch. He also stipulated in the contract with the government that the advertising matter would be set in 10- and 12-point type—nearly twice the size normally used in legal advertising. In the year after this special law was passed, Ottley's *Home Journal* collected more than $111,000 from the government on vouchers signed by him as president of the senate for payment to himself as publisher. At the same time Ottley's newspaper was printing government advertising at $8 an inch, it also was printing the *Legislative Journal* and other accounts of official proceedings, months after the fact, at $5 and $6 a column inch. (Ottley also apparently turned to his printing press on occasions when he needed a little extra money. In 1966, the *Home Journal* collected $6,720 for printing legislative records for the years 1955 and 1959). When Comptroller Ross later questioned the propriety of the special advertising legislation, a suit was filed against Ottley and his newspaper to get back $90,000 of the money paid. The suit is still unsettled. However, legal advertising and other government printing contracts are now put out for competitive bidding.

Senator Ottley, re-elected in 1970 for the fourteenth time, today is chairman of the legislature's all-powerful finance committee. He has a double-locked office in the legislative hall, its door always closed, and a spiral staircase leading from it to the only private entrance to the building.

An old associate tried to explain him to me. "He's a strange man," he said. "Sure, he made money out of that advertising contract, but it wasn't all that much. I think he was just trying to hurt the *Daily News.* I doubt if Earle Ottley has made all that much money out of being the boss. What he always wanted was power. Funny thing, when he got it, he retreated behind those 'shades' he wears all the time because of his bad eyes. Then he built that house of his in Tutu and put a high wall around it and guards it with three dogs and doesn't see anybody very much any more."

While some of them were feathering their own nests and those of their relatives and friends, Virgin Islands legislators were careful to throw occasional worms to the populace. In many cases, the worms were fat ones, for probably nowhere under the American flag can selective largesse be handed out more generously. For example, the Virgin Islands legislature pays the bill for most of the private organizations that on the mainland are supported largely by donations. No one in St. Thomas has to use the line "I gave at the office" to a fund-drive solicitor. A few random appropriations in 1970: Boy Scouts, $30,000; Girl Scouts, $30,000; St. Thomas Golf Association, $6,000; Inter-island tour by Girls' Softball League, $10,000; Carnival Committee, $12,000; Community Band, $25,000; Improvement of Race-track Facilities, $20,000; Humane Society, $20,000.* And there were many, many more handouts hidden away in financial reports under such general headings as "Other Grants and Contributions." In 1970, the Department of Conservation and Cultural Affairs—the department that gave the money to the golfers and the band —listed expenditures of nearly a quarter of a million dollars under that category.

Right through the 1960s, vast sums of easy money also went to the many experts who flocked to the Virgins in ever increasing numbers to study, survey, and draw up new plans for everything from the educational system to airports.

"We seem to have an inferiority complex about our ability to handle our own affairs," one islander observed. "I don't

---

* The 1971 Community Chest goal for St. Thomas was $25,000, most of which was raised by a one-night television auction.

oppose studies and surveys. You have to find out the facts before you can act. But I do object to spending $10 million, as we did between 1965 and 1971, on 'consultants' and then doing practically nothing with their beautifully printed and carefully detailed reports. And these people don't come cheap. The Public Utilities Commission brought in fourteen people from Washington one year and paid them $10 to $30 an hour, plus $50-a-day expenses for a couple of months. They did a report that's gathering mildew in some cubbyhole somewhere."

Until 1970 when Comptroller Ross sent Republican Secretary of the Interior Walter J. Hickel a stinging report on the financial management of the Virgin Islands that, in one of its milder passages, said "a large portion" of these consulting services "could have been performed through utilization of the skills and facilities available within the local government," the freewheeling hiring of mainland experts by the Paiewonsky regime had been questioned but once. In late 1968, without competitive bidding or even examination of the costs involved, a whopping $550,000 contract was awarded to the noted Los Angeles planner and landscape engineer Lawrence Halprin, the man who advised the Kennedys and the Johnsons on landscaping of the White House and who had helped Ladybird Johnson with her beautification plans for Washington, D.C. The contract called for drawing up a master plan for the physical needs of the islands and was to be paid for from special oil royalty funds earmarked largely for conservation and environmental development. Use of the royalty funds had to be approved by the Secretary of the Interior, then Stewart L. Udall. Udall gave his approval. Shortly after Paiewonsky resigned, in February, 1969, his interim successor, Cyril E. King, as acting governor, questioned the validity of the contract. It was later abrogated, but not before $171,875 had been paid to Halprin. The present Re-

publican administration of Governor Melvin H. Evans is
suing to get the money back.

*　*　*

The Virgin Islands legislature reached the zenith of its
operations in the period just before and just after the inauguration of President Richard M. Nixon in January, 1969. It
was obvious, of course, that Governor Paiewonsky, appointed
by President Kennedy and re-appointed by President Johnson, was through, and that a Republican inevitably would
replace him. That raised the highly undesirable possibility
of vetoes by a Republican governor of the kind of special
legislation that was the forte of the Democratic legislature.
Under then-existing federal law, even if the legislature over-
rode the governor's veto, the veto could be—and usually
would be—upheld by the President, whose appointee the
governor was. The lawmakers worked overtime during January and early February grinding out bills by the dozens in
anticipation of Paiewonsky's departure, bills that took care
of a lot of people's special interests and provided money to a
number of government departments whose faulty accounting
practices had them in financial holes.

The night of February 11, 1969, just hours before he left
office, Governor Paiewonsky signed sixty-six of these bills
into law. Among these measures was Act No. 2045: "To fix
the Effective Date of the Establishment of the Virgin Islands
Port Authority." The effective date was crowded February
11, in the last hours of which the governor also appointed
120 persons to various government boards and commissions
and, by executive order, put all "unclassified" government
employees—holders of political jobs—under the protective
cover of the islands' equivalent of the Civil Service.

The law that Act No. 2405 put into operation had been
signed by Paiewonsky on Christmas Eve, 1968, but since it
involved the use of former federal property it also required

the approval of the Secretary of the Interior. Stewart Udall gave his approval on January 16, 1969, four days before he left office, the legislation to which Udall gave his imprimatur was a real Christmas gift, establishing what amounted to a government within a government. The purpose of this Authority was: "to establish, acquire, construct, develop, and improve, own, operate, and manage any and all types of air terminals, marine terminals, and *industrial, commercial, residential, and recreational developments.*" Among the enterprises covered by the latter four categories were "warehouses, quarries, cement block plants, sewage disposal plants, public dumps, parking areas, resale outlets, hotels, motels, apartments, guest houses, restaurants, office buildings, and related activities."

To finance this bizarre package, the Authority was authorized to sell $65 million in general obligation bonds, three times the existing bonded indebtedness of the Virgin Islands government, with a provision that the General Accounting Office later observed "permitted the use of income-producing properties as a lien; thus, in the event of default, bondholders could take over the properties and operate them for personal gain." The Act also gave the Authority the right of eminent domain, protection against injunctions, and the status of a corporation with legal existence separate from the government.

On that wind-up night of February 11, Paiewonsky also appointed four reliable organization Democrats to be members of the Authority's board of directors. The following day, John L. Maduro, president of the senate and, of course, an Ottley man, appointed three more board members. One of them was Ralph Paiewonsky, who was immediately chosen the Authority's chairman.

Fifteen months later, with a Nixon-appointed governor, Melvin H. Evans, in charge and with Walter J. Hickel running the Department of the Interior, a suit was filed in their names by the U.S. Attorney for the Virgin Islands charging, with considerable truth, that the legislature had exceeded its powers "by altering the fundamental structure of the territorial government so as to infringe upon the powers vested by law in the Governor and upon the supervisory power of the Secretary of the Interior." The suit never came to trial, for in July, 1971, the legislature, which by then contained a sizable number of anti-Ottley people, changed the law, eliminating the "industrial, commercial, residential, and recreational developments" functions, the bonding authority, and protection from the injunctive process, and some time later the Justice Department dropped the action. The Authority now has jurisdiction only over airports and marine facilities and has been forced to return hundreds of acres of government land that it had acquired.

Looking back, a long-time continental resident called the episode "the most brazen among all the brazen things Ralph Paiewonsky and Earle Ottley ever tried to pull off."

"It would have given the machine control of just about anything it wanted, from housing to the ball park, without any kind of public voice and without any means of holding the directors accountable for what they did. For instance, there was not even anything in the law to provide for the directors' removal, no matter what they might have arranged, except abolition of the Authority by the legislature that created it. If things hadn't been changed, the gang would have been in clover. It would have had something like an oligarchy, with all of the benefits going to those on the inside."

One of the principal aims behind passage of the Port Authority Act was to give Paiewonsky and a group of supporters a free hand with one of their pet projects, the construction of a new airport for St. Thomas. Present facilities at Harry S Truman Airport are inadequate, and landing there in a Boeing 727 medium jet is something of an adventure. The strip is short and faced at the far end by a 200-foot hill. The Port Authority's plan, already drawn up before passage of the Act establishing it, was to build a field capable of accommodating 747s at a place called Mangrove Lagoon, near the southeast end of the island, about five miles by road from the present airport.

The site chosen is a sizable area of unspoiled shallow water and wetlands—one of the few coastal areas the island's developers had not yet penetrated. It was owned by the federal government under the provisions of the Territorial Submerged Lands Act. Even so, as with the legislation establishing the Port Authority, outgoing Secretary Udall raised no barriers to what the Paiewonsky group wanted to do. Three days before he had to vacate his suite in the Department of the Interior building, with a view of the Lincoln Memorial and the Washington Monument, Secretary Udall approved giving 110 acres of the lagoon to the Virgin Islands Port Authority for the airport.

Udall's eager successor "Wally" Hickel, got in the way of the project. He suspended Interior's gift of the Mangrove Lagoon site. Later, according to the Washington *Post,* the Department of the Interior asked the Justice Department to investigate the whole airport matter—and to check as well on Udall's connections with Lawrence Halprin, the landscape engineer whose master plan for St. Thomas Cyril King had challenged, and with Henry Kimelman, a St. Thomas politician-entrepreneur who had become a special assistant to Udall in 1967.* According to the *Post,* Kimelman, while he was Udall's assistant, had attended a number of meetings in 1968 involving the airport site and had supported putting it at Mangrove Lagoon "despite a written promise from Udall to Senator Gordon Allott (R., Colo.) that Kimelman would not work on Virgin Islands matters while in the Interior De-

* Kimelman headed the finance committee during Senator George McGovern's campaign for the Democratic presidential nomination.

partment." Kimelman was part-owner of land very close to the present noisy airport and would undoubtedly have benefited by its being moved elsewhere.

After the Nixon administration took office, Udall joined with Halprin and Kimelman to form a consulting firm in Washington known as the Overview Group, with Kimelman as president, Udall as chairman of the board, and Halprin as chairman of the executive committee. A lengthy investigation of this arrangement and the airport matter was made by the Federal Bureau of Investigation—according to Udall, at the direct urging of Secretary Hickel—but nothing actionable was found. Udall called a press conference to describe what had been going on and to refute the charges of conflict of interest implicit in the investigation.

Whatever the merits and motives of Hickel's action, it had a strong smell of partisan politics about it. (Various Washington sources claim that the investigation prevented Udall from running for the U.S. Senate in his home state of Arizona, as he had planned. The FBI's clean bill of health was delivered just five days after the final date for filing for the election.) The political overtones deflected attention—possibly Hickel's own attention—from the really important issue involved in the airport plan. This was the serious environmental threat it posed to one of the last primitive places on St. Thomas.

Ironically, among the strongest critics of the scheme on the basis of its environmental hazards was Ralph Paiewonsky's own brother, Isidor.

Except for a strong family resemblance, the Paiewonsky brothers are very different men. Ralph has been involved in island politics since shortly after he came home from New York University in the 1930s. Isidor has "run the store"—the money-coining A. H. Riise Company—from the beautiful high-ceilinged second-floor rooms on Main Street that had been the Isaac Paiewonsky family's home.

Early in the development years, Isidor became troubled about what was happening to the beauty and the ecology of the islands. In 1969, he and other conservationists were especially appalled by the Mangrove Lagoon airport project. They said that it would destroy the delicate chain of marine life embracing the wetland area itself and the reefs and shores beyond it. When the proponents of the new airport came up with a complex plan to build large tunnels under the proposed runway that would, they claimed, permit the tidal flow to continue unchecked and, combined with a system of dikes and settling ponds, protect the marine life of the lagoon, the conservationists were far from convinced. They called the plan "grandiose and impractical." Nor were they impressed by an additional offer to have a marine biologist and a coastal engineer on the job to ensure against ecological damage.

The two sides, with Ralph Paiewonsky on one, Isidor on the other, had no meeting ground. Their differences could not have been made more clear than they were in "The St. Thomas Airport Story," a statement put out by the proponents of the project in the summer of 1970. Under the heading "Ecology," the text read:

> It is important for everyone to be concerned about the quality of our environment and it is imperative that they understand that in the hierarchy of life man stands above all other forms. The balance of nature, must, therefore, always favor man. It then becomes obvious that ecological decisions must be made on a systems basis rather than fragmented into sub-systems.

"I guess all you can say is, 'Forgive them; they know not what they do,'" one conservationist observed. "But that's not enough, is it? That kind of attitude is just what got us into the environmental mess we have."

A concerned St. Thomas businessman, like Isidor Paiewonsky a troubled booster of the islands, told me in November, 1971, "Everything else aside, it's probably a good thing if we don't build a new airport, anyway. We haven't caught up to what we have in the way of the tourist trade, with all the cruise ships and the plane traffic we've got already. And if we can't handle what we've now got, what could we possibly do with the hordes that would come off the 747s? More building, maybe. But where? More services? We don't have enough as it is.

"Here on St. Thomas, we're completely dependent on tourists. And you have to keep them coming, and they won't keep coming if you don't keep them happy. It's past time for us to level off and take a look at what we're doing before we try to get any bigger."

Happily, a combination of the environmentalists' protests, Interior's (belated) stay on the use of the wetlands, the complexity of the construction necessary, and, importantly, the enormous cost involved seems to have stymied the airport project. Out at Mangrove Lagoon, the smell along its swampy edges is of the decay of organic matter from which microscopic sea creatures get their sustenance, creatures on which larger creatures live, and so on and up the ecological ladder. The shallow tide laps in, untunneled, as it has since St. Thomas emerged from the sea in those violent upheavals eons ago. And the people of this steep-sloped twenty-four-square-mile island do not, at least for now, have to cope with the packed human cargoes of Boeing 747s and other big jets that a new airport would have added to the hundreds of thousands of visitors who, month in, month out, swarm in to chase fun in the sun, shopping bags in hand.

6. St. Croix: Smoke Stacks and Social Tensions

It takes eighteen minutes to fly across the forty miles of Caribbean separating Charlotte Amalie from Christiansted, St. Croix's largest town, by Grumman "Goose," a World War II–vintage amphibious airplane, but the change in scene in those eighteen minutes is such that the sister islands might well be hundreds of miles apart.

Where have all the tourists gone? Where is all the traffic that daylong fills Charlotte Amalie's streets? Where are the shopping bags and the overt commercialism? Where is the slovenliness so apparent on St. Thomas? Crucians will shrug off the questions. This is a different island from St. Thomas —as different today as it was in the eighteenth and nineteenth centuries and in the early twentieth. So they say.

The physical differences are obvious. To begin with, Christiansted remains a very small town, seemingly untouched by the development years. Back from the harbor's edge, dominated by the neatly kept, freshly painted Fort Christianvaern, is a park and a broad plaza edged with buildings from the days of the Danish West India and Guinea Company, now part of a "National Historic Site." Past the plaza are blocks of handsome colonnaded buildings in pastel pinks, yellows, and greens with the high-peaked roofs that collect rainwater so well and help to moderate the heat of the tropical sun. A pleasant walk on a shaded sidewalk from the harbor is the large, graceful, yellow and white Government House, which the governor uses on his visits to St. Croix—a building with real character that shames everything occupied by the government of the Virgin Islands on St. Thomas.

The town's small permanent population is not much more than three thousand, and that is a surprising 40 per cent *smaller* than it was in 1960. St. Croix too has had its flight to the "suburbs." The regular residents and the residential winter visitors share the streets with only a tiny number of one-day trippers, and no cruise-ship passengers. The broad harbor of Christiansted could accommodate eighteenth- and nineteenth-century sailing ships, but reefs and shoals and shallow water close the port to ocean liners. Nearly all of the few one-day trippers who come to Christiansted arrive on the "Goose" from Charlotte Amalie, or by other planes that put into the island's Alexander Hamilton Airport, about seven miles from town. The majority of the visitors to Christiansted and the rest of St. Croix come to stay for a while. Though far less visible than the tourists in St. Thomas, they contribute substantially to the island's prosperity. For example, although more than three times as many people visit St. Thomas as St. Croix, the spending on hotels, in bars and restaurants, and on other tourist services is only 15 per cent more on St. Thomas. (Gift-shop and liquor-store sales on St. Thomas outstrip those on St. Croix by more than four to one.) St. Croix better fits the relaxed vacationer's idea of a place to spend some time in tropical ease, a place to sit on a hotel balcony with a drink and watch the boats in the harbor, or to loll under a palm tree on the beach, a world removed from the bustle of the mainland and the commercial busyness that is an integral part of St. Thomas.

But away from the charm of the downtown area of Christiansted and the hotels by the water and the beaches, it becomes apparent that St. Croix, too, has problems, and that these problems are even more complex than those of the capital island. Even Christiansted has its slums and depressed areas and an ugly and unplanned "strip development" of service stations, repair shops, drive-ins, and stores along the main highway just outside of town. Elsewhere, dust, fumes, and smoke from new industries and power and desalination plants befoul much of the island's air. Extensive harbor dredging has endangered reefs on St. Croix's south shore. "Crime in the streets" arouses fear and anger in local residents—although there is nothing that comes close to the mainland meaning of the phrase. Possibly more than a quarter of the population consists of Spanish-speaking Puerto Ricans. Although many of them have lived on St. Croix for a generation or more, they are far from being assimilated into the island's fabric. And there are separated whites as well—the self-separated relative newcomers who are the managers and technicians and top-level artisans of the island's new industries. Most of them live in all-white enclaves, and they have brought a kind of "redneck" prejudice with them to the Caribbean. Among the natives, there is resentment against the hard-working Puerto Ricans and the better-paid whites (as well as against their fellow Virgin Islanders on St. Thomas, whom the Crucians claim, with some justification, have more and better government jobs available to them).

From the air, St. Croix looks as though it might be a place for agriculture. And it once was. At its northeast corner and at the east end of the island are steep hilly areas, but most of its eighty-four-square-mile area is relatively level. In 1796, at the height of plantation prosperity, more than 54 per cent of the island was planted in sugar cane. There were 114 windmills and 144 animal-driven mills engaged in grinding juice from the cane, the first step in the extraction of sugar. Many of the truncated conical stone towers of the mills still stand,

and it is considered very chic to have such a tower on one's property.

The plantation era has long since vanished. Even the cultivation of cane ceased at the beginning of the 1960s, when VICORP closed its sugar operations. But cane is persistent, and in the undulating fields between Christiansted and Frederiksted, on the western end of the island, are many large patches of it, reverted through nature's processes into what looks like high, reedy grass. Many other patches have disappeared beneath the blades of bulldozers and scrapers tearing up the reddish-brown earth to make way for real estate subdivisions. The relatively flat land lends itself to the kind of development that has been going on in mainland suburbia since World War II. Subdivisions are springing up everywhere, complete with that basic accoutrement of suburbia, the shopping center, indistinguishable from its mainland counterpart: Acres of paved parking area surrounded by Sears, Drug Fair, Colonel Sanders Kentucky Fried Chicken, McDonald's, Grand Union, Texaco, etc.

A large proportion of the people who move into the developments and shop in the supermarkets are new-style continentals, not the rich who buy hillside or seaside property—preferably with a windmill—or the kind of retired people found on Florida's West Coast. ("This place," a St. Croix real estate man said, "is no longer the lovely tropical paradise where you could retire on $10,000 a year.") Many of the newcomers describe themselves as "semi-retired." They have come to make a second career in pursuits ranging from shopkeeping to charter-boat operation. Others are well-paid younger people with needed skills and training—some of whom, if they are working for mainland-based companies, even get what amounts to "overseas pay."

It is in the younger group that most of the racism is found, racism demonstrated not by outright animosity (which would be a very difficult attitude to maintain in a community where the blacks are in the majority and hold power) but by unheeding social discrimination.

J. Anthony Lukas, in the *New York Times Magazine* of April 18, 1971, told of a continental woman who tried to organize an interracial committee on St. Croix to raise funds for the Red Cross. The wife of a company official newly arrived from the mainland asked, "Won't that make it difficult for you to have meetings? Where are you going to hold them?"

"Your house, maybe."

"Oh, no. I don't have Negroes in my house."

A woman instructor at the St. Croix branch of the College of the Virgins told me, "We don't mind these people coming in from the mainland and sticking together the way they do out at the Hess refinery and Harvey Alumina, with their own clubs and social life, but when they bring their social attitudes into public places like bars and restaurants here in town and practically freeze you out with prejudice you can *feel,* that is something else. Why, in some of the places where the new continentals hang out, the natives are treated as if this were Richmond, Virginia."

Native Crucians are confused by the unexpected experience of meeting overt racial prejudice in public places. Since the island historically was overwhelmingly black and almost all the blacks were field hands, social contact between the races was very small. The U.S. Navy, when it arrived, set up an all-white tennis club and an all-white country club, which must have seemed like a deliberate snub to the few blacks who had become local businessmen and social leaders. The navy's rule, however, lasted only fourteen years, and during its later years and the early years of civilian rule—a period of dreadful economic distress—many of the small white population joined the thousands of natives who fled to the lesser evil of the mainland Depression. Almost all of those few whites who remained were native-born landowners from the days of Danish rule who maintained their traditional separatism, which everybody was used to and took for granted, keeping themselves aloof even from the navy. Thus, after World War II, the over-all social situation was much the same as it had been before the United States took over the island: a large black population and a tiny group of white landowners who lived to themselves as they always had.

Mrs. William G. Thayer, Jr., who came to Frederiksted from New York in 1948 with her late husband, described what the place was like then: "There were only about a hundred old white residents on the island besides the few people like ourselves who had come down from the mainland in retirement. 'The royal families' these old residents were called—though the natives used the term as one of derision. But these white families, Danes and British mostly, didn't know about the derision and sort of believed they *were* 'royal families,' even if they didn't have much but their land.

"The first party we gave after we finished restoring an old plantation house at Butler Bay, we invited all of the people we had got to know. It was a mixed party, of course, but when the 'royal families' people arrived, they were shocked. They were appalled. We were not trying to be 'liberal' or anything like that. It just seemed to be the thing to do since we had moved into the community, had met new people— some of whom we liked and some of whom we didn't—and just went ahead as we would have anywhere. But the 'royal families' never forgave us for it."

The distance between the attitudes of the parochial old whites and people like Mrs. Thayer who came to St. Croix in the years before the boom is no greater—perhaps not so great—as that between those who came to the islands not to earn money but to enjoy spending it in tropical surroundings and those who come to make a killing. Island ways did not bother the first wave of immigrants as they do many of the newcomers. And, perhaps more important, there were not many of them—not enough to call a wave, in fact.

There *has* been a wave in the past decade, however. The continental population of St. Croix, according to the 1970 census, increased fourfold to more than four thousand. (The continental population on St. Thomas increased about 2.5 times during the 1960–70 period.) This large number of "new whites" combined with the very large and already resident Puerto Rican population, numbering about four thousand in 1960 and now probably eight thousand or more, is a long-range threat to the native blacks' majority. In the 1970 Census, only about 60 per cent of the island's U.S. citizens were born in the territory. (Slightly more than one third of the counted population were nonvoting aliens.)

Puerto Ricans began coming to St. Croix many years ago, but the influx grew rapidly during and after World War II. A large number were migrants from the island of Vieques, from which they were virtually evicted by the U.S. military in the ticklish days of the successful German submarine campaign in the Atlantic and the Caribbean, just after Pearl Harbor. St. Croix, then still agricultural, suited the Puerto Ricans better than did St. Thomas, and when agriculture waned most of them became artisans, small shopkeepers, and technicians. But they kept to themselves and, as in New York City and elsewhere on the mainland, retained their strong ties to the mother country. In particular, they, like other Puerto Rican exiles, held on to their language and social organizations. There are so many children of Spanish-speaking parents in the schools of St. Croix that bilingual instruction has had to be offered in areas where the Puerto Ricans have concentrated. And bilingual medical and social services have been requested. In the 1970 election for the islands' governor and the legislature, ballots were for the first time printed in English and Spanish, and Puerto Rican voters had their choice among candidates of the *Partido Republicano Progrestista, Partido Democrata,* and *Partido I.C.M.* Until that election, the Democratic organization usually had a few tame Puerto Ricans, sort of *Tio Tomases,* on the ticket but never allowed them to play a significant part in government. However, in 1970 six of the twenty candidates for St. Croix's six seats in the legislature were Puerto Ricans. Two were elected, both Republicans, and they were elected by the votes of Puerto Ricans and continentals combined.

* * *

Before the 1960s, none of the Virgin Islands had any industry beyond the budding tourist business, rum distilling, and the making of bay rum—that one-time favorite of barbers. The situation today is much different on St. Croix, to which the development years have brought industry ranging from the very small to the very large: watch factories, textile-processing plants, and two real giants—the Harvey Alumina Corporation and the Hess Oil Company.

Under special provisions of the U.S. tariff laws, manufactured goods to which 50 per cent of value has been added in processing can be shipped duty-free from the Virgin Islands to the mainland. Fifteen watch companies, eleven of them on St. Croix, have taken advantage of the law to put together twenty-two million movements—the "works"—and ship them to watch companies in the States. They are assembled from parts made in Japan, Switzerland, West Germany, the Soviet Union, and other countries. (The watch companies imported $400,000 worth of Soviet-made springs, ratchets, balance wheels, and other parts in 1969.) Five textile mills (one on St. Thomas, four on St. Croix) process about ten million yards of woolens and other fabrics each year for duty-free shipment to the mainland under the same tariff provisions. Both the watch and the textile industries benefit from the islands' Industrial Incentive Program, with its generous subsidies and freedom from import duties and local taxes. But neither industry benefits to the degree that the big boys—Harvey and Hess—do. Both of them are in special categories established by laws passed by the Virgin Islands legislature.

Harvey Alumina was first on the ground, reportedly attracted to the islands through the influence of President John F. Kennedy. On January 1, 1962, the government of the Virgin Islands, under a law passed by the legislature, agreed to allow Harvey to build a $25-million alumina-extraction plant on St. Croix and to develop a port on the south shore of the island to land the bauxite ore used in the production of alumina, the first-step product in the refining of aluminum. The government's rationale was that Harvey would "alleviate underemployment in the Virgin Islands" and "improve the quality of employment through the offering of employment involving higher skills." To meet these requirements, the agreement—which throughout leans to Harvey's side—required that the plant employ local labor, but the specific wording was that "not less than 75 per cent of persons employed in the operation and maintenance of the plant and related facilities shall be legal residents of the Virgin Islands." In his 1970 report, Comptroller Ross noted that only 20 of the 471 persons then employed were Virgin Islanders, and 65 per cent of the remainder were imported aliens, who, by the letter of the law, may have been "legal residents" but were certainly not alleviating local unemployment.

This first big industry brought St. Croix problems unforeseen, or ignored, by the Virgin Islands government. Bauxite is a light-textured reddish dirt that is picked up and blown around by even mild breezes. An aluminum-company official in Washington says that his company has had "real problems" with the ore at its stateside plants and, although it is now storing it in bins, is still getting complaints from nearby communities. Harvey stored its bauxite in piles, open to the stiff tradewinds, and Crucians soon began complaining about the "red dust" that coats everything to leeward, including the private planes of the affluent at nearby Alexander Hamilton Airport. Also, the extraction process leaves behind large amounts of slightly caustic gunk, called in the trade "red mud," that must be stored somewhere. Harvey, like other aluminum companies, stores it in huge man-made ponds that sometimes leak into nearby waters. Harvey is directly on the water, or at least it was until it filled in the shallows of Krause Lagoon, an area much like St. Thomas's Mangrove Lagoon, where it built its private harbor—now designated on Coast and Geodetic Service Chart 905 as Port Harvey.

Former officials of the Virgin Islands government who supported Harvey's advent to St. Croix have since had second thoughts. One man, a native who backed the project, told me, "They really sold us a bill of goods." Another, who was involved in Harvey's negotiations with the ineffective Virgin Islands Planning Board, said, "Harvey gave the board a glowing picture of what the place was going to look like— buildings painted in colors that would blend with the landscape, and a lot of planting of trees and shrubs to break up the industrial bleakness—something like an 'industrial park.' But there it stands, without a tree around it and all the buildings built, of course, of aluminum, glaring in the sun. If you are an airplane pilot, you can find your way here just by looking for the reflection. They never did a thing they said they were going to do."

Harvey's red dust, raw earth, gunk, glare, and name remain, but Leo M. Harvey has left. Beginning in 1968, the giant conglomerate Martin-Marietta began buying Harvey stock and now controls the company, although Harvland, a Harvey affiliate, kept control of two thousand acres of land —almost all it had acquired in 1961. Judging from current prices, the land is possibly worth between $10 million and $15 million.

The Hess story is more complex, the oil industry being what it is.

The company, a large fuel-oil distributor, is controlled by Leon Hess, who in old baseball terms is a Class AAA League Paul Getty. His present corporation, Amerada-Hess, ranks 89th among the blue-chip firms in *Fortune* magazine's annual listing of the five hundred largest American industrial corporations. (In the 1971 compilation, Amerada-Hess ranked 111th.) Sales, as reported by the magazine, amounted to nearly $1.35 billion.

Like Paiewonsky, Hess is the son of a Lithuanian immigrant, who, coincidentally, came to the United States the same year Paiewonsky's father emigrated to the Virgin Islands. Hess built his company to its present eminence from a tiny 615-gallon tank truck he used to deliver fuel oil in Asbury Park, N.J., in the 1930s. (He holds a 25 per cent interest in the New York Jets football team and 13 per cent of the Monmouth Park Jockey Club, which runs that New Jersey racetrack.)

In 1965, Hess, whose company already had refineries at Port Reading, near Perth Amboy, N.J., and Corpus Christi, Texas, was looking for broader fields of operation. According to an article in *Fortune*, in January, 1970, he toyed with the idea of building a refinery in the Bahamas but was persuaded by David Rockefeller, president of the Chase Manhattan Bank and one of Hess Oil's principal bankers, to look into possibilities in the Virgins, where the Rockefeller family owned a lot of real estate, including four thousand acres on St. Croix and the Caneel Bay Plantation on St. John.

The Virgins had a lot of inducements to offer Hess. The territory is the only area under U.S. jurisdiction from which foreign-flag ships can be used for transportation to U.S. ports. This benefit amounts to a 25 to 45 per cent reduction in tanker rates compared to those paid by other American oil companies engaged in coastal trade. And Hess's shipments, if he moved to the Virgins, would be coastal—from the islands to his big terminal in New Jersey—serving the enormous fuel-oil market of the metropolitan New York area and beyond. There was, in addition, the Virgin Islands subsidy program.

In December, 1947, shortly after he got out of the army, Leon Hess had married a divorcée whose maiden name was Norma Wilentz, the daughter of David T. Wilentz, the man who had successfully prosecuted the case against Bruno Richard Hauptmann in the famous Lindbergh kidnapping trial. Wilentz was a big wheel in the northern New Jersey Democratic Party organization, and also, coincidentally, an immigrant from Lithuania. Through his father-in-law, Hess soon got on the inside of Democratic politics in New Jersey. (And national Democratic politics as well. According to *Fortune*, in 1968 he "loaned the Humphrey-for-President organization $100,000; the money has not yet been repaid.") When the Virgin Islands refinery idea arose, he called then-Governor Richard J. Hughes, a good Johnson-style Democrat, who in turn called Governor Paiewonsky. These conversations led to a visit by Hess to the Virgin Islands in July, 1965. Two days after he arrived, Leon Hess had bought 824 acres of land near the Harvey property with access to Krause Lagoon from a native widow, Mrs. Ansetta de Chabert, for nearly $2 million. He later picked up two smaller tracts for about $1,500,000. The Virgin Islands legislature then came through with a special bill giving Hess a sixteen-year subsidy, similar to that given to Harvey, because "it is essential to the continued progress, prosperity, and stability of the Virgin Islands economy that dependence on tourism be relieved through the establishment of industrial operations capable of providing and sustaining large scale employment."

The bill passed on September 1, 1965; on December 15,

1965, a frenetic building program began. *Fortune* reported, "Hess, as if driven by demons, visited the construction site every week, personally supervising and masterminding every phase of the work." Within ten months, the refinery was producing.

The arrangements made between Hess and the Virgin Islands government were largely similar to those made three years before with Harvey: a specified investment—in Hess's case $70 million, of which $30 million was to be spent on a petrochemical plant; assurance that at least 75 per cent of the refinery's employees would be "legal residents of the Virgin Islands"; and the promise that Hess would be allowed to build its own port, in this instance to supply its refinery with crude oil. A careful reading of the nine laws and two resolutions passed by the legislature during the Paiewonsky-Ottley period in support of the Hess proposal can only lead to the belief that the Hess lawyers had a hand in their drafting. Not only was Hess granted the return of 75 per cent of income taxes, but all Virgin Islands residents who invested in Hess stock would receive a 75 per cent return of taxes on Hess dividends, making the stock almost as good as municipal bonds. The contractors and subcontractors building the Hess plant were granted freedom from "all excise taxes on building materials." And an act was passed stating that the basic agreement was contractual in nature and expressly declaring that "the Government will not adopt any legislation impairing or limiting the obligations of these contracts." Like Harvey, Hess was granted not only tax relief but also customs relief, the latter—as with Harvey—in full.

Topping all this, the Virgin Islands government—Governor Paiewonsky and the legislature—also agreed to recommend to the Department of the Interior that Hess be given a special daily quota of "25,000 barrels of finished petroleum products" (read gasoline) for its own importation into the United States—this "to promote the general public interest

by vastly and substantially assisting the economic development and well-being of the Virgin Islands." The special
quota, described as "vital and crucial to the islands' further
development," was as vital and crucial to Hess, for in the
production of fuel oil, the larger part of Hess's money-mak-
ing sales, it is also necessary to produce gasoline and other
"top products," those that are more volatile than the heavier
oils and are the first things that come out of distillation of
crude. The quota would provide Hess with its market for
gasoline.

A year after the St. Croix refinery began producing, Hess
got its quota from the Department of the Interior, although
the amount was reduced to 15,000 barrels a day for a ten-year
period, not the sixteen years asked for, and the terms of the
allocation agreement, signed by Secretary Udall on December 12, 1967, were stern in tone: Hess was to pay a royalty of
$7,500 a day (50 cents a barrel) into a special Virgin Islands
Conservation Fund; it was not only to employ 75 per cent
"local residents" from the start but was required to increase
the proportion gradually to 90 per cent by the end of 1972,
and not less than half of the refinery's output was to be produced from low-sulfur Western Hemisphere crude. The
Virgin Islands legislature established a Department of Conservation and Cultural Affairs to administer the Hess contributions to the conservation fund, $2.7 million a year to be used
for "air and water pollution control, sewage treatment and
disposal, sewage systems, preservation of historical and archi-
tectural heritages of the Virgin Islands, and beautification."

The Hess association with the conservation fund is not
without irony. The company, before construction began, obtained from the Department of the Interior a permit to
dredge a thirty-five-foot-deep channel, turnaround area, and
berthing facilities for its tankers, and the right to use land
created with dredged materials for a rental of $600 a year
per acre—$50 a month. More than sixty acres of this made-

land are in use. As in the construction of Port Harvey, a cut had to be made through a coral formation known as Long Reef, with the total channel length and its protecting dike extending seaward nearly a mile. The dredging, which was still in progress early in 1972, produced considerable silting, to the great distress of Virgin Islands conservationists, who can do nothing about it since the operation has been authorized by the Interior Department.

Jean Larson, a member of the staff of the Caribbean Research Institute stationed on St. Croix, showed me dozens of color aerial photos taken over a period of months in which the yellowish brown stain of silt stood out starkly against the deep blue of the Caribbean and extended, in some of the pictures, for the more than eleven miles from Hess's operations to Sandy Point, the southeastern tip of the island.

The institute, which is associated with the College of the Virgin Islands, has made an extensive study of the effects of water turbidity and silting on sea life, in particular, coral. In a paper printed in the Caribbean Conservation Association's "Environmental Newsletter," David I. Grigg, a CRI research assistant, wrote:

> The primary effect of chronic turbidity is to cut down the amount of light which reaches plants on the bottom. Plants are the primary producers of food. In addition to food, they provide refuge for many species of animals. Without some minimum amount of light (the amount varies with the kind of plant), plants die and then the whole associated community is destroyed because of the loss of food or refuge. Of particular importance in these waters, however, is the effect of light loss on corals and other related reef organisms. Corals are animals, but the reef-building forms particularly depend on the survival of symbiotic unicellular algae (*zooanthellae*) which live within the coral tissues. There is a poorly understood nutrient relationship between the plant and animal, but it is known that when these corals lose their *zooanthellae* they become unhealthy and die.

Turbidity is not something that quickly clears away. Grigg noted that "in all the operations which we have observed, enough of these fine materials remain in suspension to noticeably reduce submarine visibility for up to two years after the finish of dredging." The siltation that occurs, when the suspended particles of sand and clay finally settle on the bottom, also can continue for some time after dredging and may occur at far-removed sites. "Its effects can be catastrophic for sessile organisms [those that cannot move]," Grigg wrote. "If the rate of fallout is too great many sedentary organisms, particularly corals, are literally smothered because their ability to cleanse themselves is overloaded."

"Most of the offshore formation along the southern coast is coral," Larson told me, "and the water is shallow. We don't know for sure yet what has happened to the reefs, but they certainly are not being helped."

Since coral reefs play a vital part in protecting beaches from erosion, the death of the reefs would obviously endanger St. Croix beaches, as does the dredging itself. Any threat to these beaches, which, unlike those of St. Thomas, are numerous and in many cases open to all comers, seems to many Crucians a shameless thing for the Virgin Islands government and the Department of the Interior to have permitted.

Damage to the reefs is not the only bad effect, environmentally speaking. The Hess Oil Plant, unlike Harvey, has been made as attractive as an oil refinery with its tanks and pipes and stills and cracking towers can be. It has been extensively landscaped and the area surrounding it kept in good order. But it is still a refinery. High stacks spew smoke twenty-four hours a day, and waste gases burn atop a half-dozen high exhaust pipes. To a layman who has seen oil refineries in many parts of the world, the amount of emissions appears excessive. Moreover, there have been incidents of oil spills from tankers fouling nearby beaches.

An anti-organization senator, Alexander Moorhead, Jr., of St. Croix, who was elected in 1970, has been riding Hess hard on the air and water pollution. "I am not persuaded by those who have said that pollution is a necessary evil in the course of economic progress," he said. "I am of the opinion that air and water pollution by industrial plants are the result of shortcuts to business profits." Hess, he said, must become "more keen to the people of these islands and the islands' fragile and priceless beauty." Under prodding by Moorhead and others, in 1971—five years after it began production— Hess installed gas-collecting equipment and converted its heaters for naphtha, a cleaner-burning fuel which can be obtained in the refining process.

Senatorial complaints about air and water pollution have not been the only official criticisms leveled at Hess. In November, 1970, after the Justice Department had told Stewart Udall it had found no reason to bring charges of conflict-of-interest against him in other matters, the Nixon Department of the Interior took a look at the Hess agreements with the Virgin Islands and Udall's order giving the company a 15,000-barrel-a-day import quota. Investigators visited St. Croix, and, some months later, Interior's Oil Import Administration (OIA) wrote to Leon Hess pointing out that the company had not met two important requirements set forth in the allocation agreement and that OIA proposed to revoke the allocation.

One of the unmet requirements was that $30 million was to have been spent to build a petrochemical plant of a type "which will afford maximum employment on the islands." (The allocation proclamation said, "This subject action would serve substantially to promote employment of, substantially to upgrade opportunities for employment of Virgin Islanders, or substantially to increase revenues received by the Virgin Islanders.")

OIA's second point was that Hess had not met the requirement of employing, by 1970, not less than 80 per cent of legal residents. (Hess in April, 1970, had refused to give Comptroller Ross a breakdown of the origins of its then-400 employees. However, published reports said that only about 10 per cent of Hess's work force were native Virgin Islanders.) Hess replied to OIA that it had not built the petrochemical plant because a boom in that field had produced a surfeit of petrochemical plants, and besides, it had invested more than $100 million in its St. Croix operation and was still expanding. As for the "legal residents" stipulation, the company said it had more than 70 per cent and was pushing to increase the proportion. A large majority of the "legal residents" working for Hess are continentals imported by the company. To objections that this policy evades the intent of the laws and agreements supposedly designed to give jobs to Virgin Islanders, Hess argues that it has extensively advertised available jobs locally and maintains a training school for new employees on St. Croix. But the company has not been 100 per cent forthright.

A college-trained native Crucian who had come back to his home island after working for ten years for a New York engineering firm went to the Hess personnel office before the refinery went into full production, looking for a job. "I have a degree in physics," he said. "The personnel manager looked at my papers and my experience, then he said to me, 'Well, you know this is a refinery and we need process engineers. You have a degree in physics and you should be working for the Atomic Energy Commission. You're wasting your time here on St. Croix, you know.' " The Crucian said, "You have a situation where there are no locals, as far as I know, in supervisory jobs. They had no intention of training local people. What they are saying is that the local people can't learn their processes. One of these days that attitude's going to backfire."

Holding onto the 15,000-barrels-a-day allocation (about 230 million gallons a year) is important to the Hess operation, according to an OIA official. "There is a glut of gasoline worldwide," he said, "but not in the States, where there is always a market. The value of the quota to Hess is that in the production of heavy oils—the larger part of Hess's business—it's necessary to get rid of the lighter products, because if they fill up your storage tanks, there's no place to put the heavier stuff. So that makes those 15,000 barrels so much cream that they otherwise wouldn't have."

This official also noted that Hess sells most of its production within its own organization, and "with the tax break they get in the Virgin Islands, they can use the place to pay taxes, which amount to only 25 cents on the dollar, in real terms, because of the 75 per cent tax subsidy they get."

The subsidies paid to Hess by the Virgin Islands have skyrocketed as production has increased, totaling nearly $16 million for the period from July 1, 1970, to June 30, 1971, a sum roughly equal to one seventh of the money the Virgin Islands government spent on its operations that year. It also amounted to 65 per cent of all income taxes and 93 per cent of all import duties returned to 73 companies then benefiting from the Industrial Incentive Plan. From the time the refinery went on stream in 1966 through the end of 1971, total government subsidies paid to Hess amounted to approximately $30 million. The current annual rate of repayment is in the neighborhood of $20 million. And, if rumors prevalent on St. Croix are true (the gist: "Hess plans to make its refinery here the biggest in the world"), the subsidies could get even bigger.

Finding out about future plans for the St. Croix refinery is difficult. Leon Hess does not talk for publication to anybody. *Fortune* has said, "He has an almost pathological aversion to publicity." A *Life* reporter who managed to get to see him in 1971, after weeks of persistent pushing, was told after a two-hour conversation, "This, of course, is off the record." In any event, whether or not Hess Oil Virgin Islands Corporation goes on to build the biggest refinery in the world, it has so far built a big one indeed. The only larger refinery under the American flag is Humble Oil's at Baton Rouge, Louisiana, and its capacity of 434,000 barrels a day is not all that far ahead of Hess's present 400,000 barrels a day on St. Croix. During the period when it was building and expanding in the Virgins, Hess merged with the Amerada Petroleum Company, holder of huge oil reserves in the United States, Canada, and Libya, assuring a sure supply of crude. Before the merger in 1969, Hess's only owned source of oil was a field in Mississippi, which produced a piddling 3,500 barrels a day. Also, since the merger, Amerada-Hess has become a big investor in Alaska's North Slope, an area of enormous potential.

For Hess, the future in the Virgin Islands looks bright. But for the islands, the presumed benefits of this particular venture into industrialization seem a long way off. Any significant contribution the refinery may make to the economy cannot come until 1981, when Hess's sixteen-year subsidy period expires. Only then is the Virgin Islands treasury supposed to get its full share of the multimillion-dollar earnings. And who knows what might happen to the oil business, or, for that matter, to the corporate entity of Amerada-Hess and hard-driving Leon Hess by 1981?

Hess supporters on the islands argue that the Virgins already are getting large amounts of money—in 1971, $2.1 million in income taxes and $2.75 million in royalty payments—that they otherwise would not have received. Whether these amounts are adequate compensation for fouled air and silted reefs between now and 1981 other islanders doubt, even though the money involved is considerable.

If Hess operations and income remain at 1972 levels, more

than $20 million in additional revenue will be realized annually by the Virgin Islands government when the dough comes rolling in. That is about one quarter of all locally collected revenue in fiscal 1970. But before 1981 Hess will probably be using supertankers with the larger accompanying dangers of spills, wrecks, and accidents, such as have occurred so frequently around the world in recent years. In hurricane-prone St. Croix and the Caribbean, this could be spectacularly disastrous. To accomodate these supertankers, continued dredging will be required, with continued silting. From past performance, it can be assumed that little will be done to prevent further despoilation. Moreover, in the years until 1981, Hess obviously will not add appreciably to Crucian employment. Whether or not the islanders are reluctant to work in industry ("Crucians don't like shift work," a Hess supervisor told me), the basic purpose of the law passed to allow the refinery's construction has been lost sight of. The Virgin Islands, in brief, now have a largely uncontrolled giant within their gates.

The lonely voice of Comptroller Ross in a report to the Secretary of the Interior and the governor of the Virgin Islands noted that not only did Hess and Harvey have few natives on their payrolls but the whole Industrial Incentive Program had fallen far short of its goal of providing jobs. In April, 1970, he said, of 4,725 persons working for subsidized companies from which he had received information, only 780—or slightly more than 16 per cent—were native Virgin Islanders. Ross questioned the whole operation of the Industrial Incentive Program:

> There have been no cost vs. benefit studies made before approval of grants to tax exemptions and subsidy, and there are indications that certain grantees receive benefits in excess of their value to the Virgin Islands. This is particularly true in the case of those businesses which require the importation of large numbers of workers from outside the Virgin Islands,

who, because of the acute shortage of housing, must live under substandard conditions, since the Government has not made it mandatory that employers provide adequate housing prior to importation of such workers. Social problems and economic problems of serious consequence have resulted, including a sharp rise in crime, overcrowding of schools, and a breakdown in educational standards.

In reports published in 1970 and 1971, Ross also questioned the legality of the acts passed by the Virgin Islands legislature for the benefit of Hess and Harvey, citing 48 U.S.C. 1471, which forbids passage of special legislation in certain categories and adds, "In all other cases where a general law can be applicable, no special law shall be enacted in any of the Territories of the United States by the Territorial Legislatures." There was a general law on the books before Hess and Harvey came along, that which established the Industrial Incentive Program, and Ross said that this law alone would have been enough. The comptroller additionally objected to the fact that Hess and Harvey, and the Virgin Islands Telephone Company, and affiliate of the giant conglomerate ITT, get back 100 per cent of customs duties paid— "favored treatment," in the comptroller's phrase, "not accorded to other grantees." All other businesses benefiting from the Industrial Incentive Program get back 90 per cent; the other 10 per cent is kept by the U.S. Treasury Department for administrative costs of its Customs Service. Hess's 10 per cent now adds up to nearly $1 million. California Representative Phillip Burton, chairman of the House Subcommittee on Territorial and Insular Affairs, pointed out at a hearing in Washington on April 20, 1971, "When Hess oil production increases, it is going to cost the Virgin Islands money."

Because of the objections raised by Comptroller Ross, the Virgin Islands government in 1971 did not return to Hess the full 100 per cent of duties paid. Hess in turn withheld its $2.75 million royalty payment to the Conservation Fund. Such scrupulous pursuit of the letter of its agreements with the Virgin Islands is not unusual for Hess. Another example: The terms of paying the tiny rental for land created by Hess dredging in Krause Lagoon were not precise, and Hess did not pay the rental—a paltry $54,000—until early April, 1971, although it had been using the made land. Payment came only after a visit to St. Croix by Representative Burton's subcommittee and some plain talk to the company's representatives on the ground by the chairman.

One persistent congressional critic of the way the islands have comported themselves is Congressman John P. Saylor of Pennsylvania, the ranking minority member of the Interior and Insular Affairs Committee, who was a member of the Subcommittee on Territorial and Insular Affairs for many of his twenty-four years in Congress and is still an *ex officio* member. Saylor dropped into Burton's subcommittee hearing in April, 1971, and, after listening to some discussion about Hess Oil and Harvey Alumina, observed, "Mr. Chairman, if you ever really get the Harvey Aluminum Company deal and the Hess Oil Company deal out in the open, some folks on your side of the aisle may have faces which are redder than any faces that have been seen around here for some time." He declined to enlarge on this statement when I talked with him some time later, but as I was leaving his office he said, "There are people down there who are still changing hundred-dollar bills they got from the Harvey deal."

It is probably unfair to fault Hess or Harvey for taking full advantage of the concessions and wide-open opportunities given them by the complaisant, perhaps uninformed, elected representatives of the Virgin Islands people and by Governor Ralph M. Paiewonsky, an appointee of two presidents of the United States. The aim of Hess, Harvey, the Virgin Islands Telephone Company, and all of the other seventy-odd companies enjoying subsidies through the liberality of the Virgin Islands is to make money for their owners, proprietors, and stockholders, and to make as much as they can within the flexible limits set on their operations. What damages the Virgin Islanders have suffered from the growth of industry, as from the extraordinary thrust of tourism and real estate development, have largely been their own fault. Not that the now-and-then attention given to the Virgin Islands by the Congress of the United States has been sufficient, nor that the Department of the Interior's virtual withdrawal from responsibility for the islands' operations has helped.

*   *   *

Early in 1970, a small group, many of them young Virgin Islanders educated on the mainland, got together on St. Croix to form the United Caribbean Association of Black People, to "create an atmosphere in which we as black people can live in harmony and complement each other rather than compete with each other." Its leader, Mario Moorhead, son of a prominent Frederiksted merchant and brother of now-Senator Alexander Moorhead and Julio Moorhead, president of the St. Croix teachers union, had worked with black militant organizations on the mainland. He had also been involved in a Washington supermarket holdup and, before the association gained much strength, was arrested on this charge by the FBI on St. Croix. He pleaded guilty to the robbery in federal court in Charlotte Amalie in May, 1970, and is now serving a seven-year sentence in the federal penitentiary at Lewisburg, Pennsylvania. But he is by no means silent. On October 20, 1971, the Virgin Islands *Daily News* published a long letter from him headed "Myth of Sand, Sun, and Surf," which concludes:

The principal problem of Virgin Islands society is foreign capital and the colonial and capitalist relations of production it fosters. It is this condition that is the source of the exploitation and hence the myriad problems of society. To fight apathy or corruption in politicians, crime in the streets, racism and discrimination, closed beaches, etc. without attacking the source is like trying to remove a shadow from a wall by painting the wall.

Mario Moorhead did not look upon Hess and Harvey and the watch companies as outright villains, although his theme throughout the long letter is "we can produce for ourselves." What he bitterly assailed was "the ideological nonsense propagandized in the Virgin Islands" that "the sun and surf are our only natural resources" and these are a "veil that shields the Real Hogs and the finance aristocracy from the wrath of the people of the Virgin Islands." The attitude embodied in Moorhead's statements, which had earlier been expressed in other statements by the United Caribbean Association, sits poorly with the Crucian continental community. (J. Anthony Lukas, in his *New York Times Magazine* article, says that white members of the St. Croix Rifle Club were deputized to patrol the streets of Christiansted on the night of the Policemen's Ball in the spring of 1970 after Moorhead had gone to jail.)

St. Croix has long been the most racially volatile of the three Virgins. It is the island where emancipation was first won, and it also is the island where, in October, 1878, frustrated plantation laborers, outraged by the contracts offered to them by their employers, went on an arson spree that is still know as the "Fire Burn." Florence Lewisohn's *Romantic History of St. Croix* says that "forty-four estates, two schools, a customshouse and police station, a big cane-weighing house at Peter's Rest, and half of Frederiksted went up in smoke." (Once-important Frederiksted even today looks rather like a Georgia village in the days before World War II.) St. Croix natives still sing about "Queen Mary," one of the leaders of the revolt.

> Queen Mary away ya go burn.
> Don' ask me nothin' 'tall
> Jus' give me a match and oil.

But the sources of internal unrest these days are much more complex than they were in Queen Mary's time. The bombastic "black power" of the United Caribbean Association, although it has frightened some continentals, is not the only or the most serious sign of the tensions that afflict the island's splintered groups of people. The latest significant protest-demonstrations held on St. Croix have been staged by non-natives—the first by Puerto Ricans and the second by alien workers. Late in February, 1971, an eight-year-old Puerto Rican girl was killed after a sexual attack. Hundreds of emotionally overwrought members of the Puerto Rican community marched on Government House in Christiansted demanding "an end to the violent crimes that have been sweeping St. Croix." A few days later, several thousand alien workers protested against the summary way the U.S. Immigration Service and the Virgin Islands police were handling the roundup of aliens illegally on the islands. They did a similar march on Government House and at the same time closed down Hess and Harvey and other businesses by their walkout.

* * *

The inseparability of St. Croix's problems of rapid industrialization and the related single-track development of land resources, environmental despoilation, the influx of new kinds of outsiders, and the division of the community into antagonistic and suspicious groups is not unique. These are all symptoms of a world disease clearly brought on—here as elsewhere—by a failure to fashion, and hold to, fair and reasonable controls on growth. But in this island setting, where two decades ago there was but a single problem—poverty, it is compellingly clear that substituting new problems for old is no way to forge a good life.

The rape of sleepy St. Croix may have been less brutal than the assault on St. Thomas by hordes of tourists cheered on by political profiteers, but it is more typical of the fate of virgin lands elsewhere. It is, in fact, as typical of what has happened around the world as what happened on St. John, the third of the American Virgins, is atypical.

7. St. John: Gentlemanly Seduction

There are two ferry routes from St. Thomas to the island of St. John. The public ferry runs from Red Hook dock on the north shore of Red Hook Bay, a deeply indented piece of sheltered water, to Cruz Bay, which is not only a bay but also the name of the only town on St. John. The Red Hook public dock is surrounded by boat yards, marinas, rusty World War II landing craft, half-sunken hulks, and beer joints. Across the water on the south shore is the U.S. National Park Service dock, reached by a better road than is found anywhere else in the Virgin Islands. It runs through well-barbered surroundings to a scrubbed-looking building decorated with instructive color-slide blow-ups of underwater life and separated from the normal hurly-burly of marine activity. Here well-heeled visitors board luxury cruisers to get to the expensive simplicity of the Rockefeller-owned Caneel Bay Plantation. The observant visitor who has used both routes is instantly aware of the problems of little St. John.

Riding the Red Hook ferry is fun—and it costs only a dollar. The fast launch is usually full of high school children returning home by the most delightful method of "busing" imaginable; St. Johnians bringing back their weekly or monthly marketing, keeping a careful eye on cartons of groceries and other purchases piled amidships; and visitors going to St. John for the day or for a stretch of $35-a-week camping in the Virgin Islands National Park. The nearly four-mile trip across sometimes boisterous Pillsbury Sound takes only about twenty minutes, and they are breathtakingly scenic minutes as the ferry speeds past rocks and cays silhouetted against the misty larger islands of the British Virgins. When the ferry pulls up to the projecting concrete wharf in Cruz Bay, frightening away thousands of tiny blue fry and the diving echelons of pelicans feeding on them, the visitor has reached a tropical place that calls up remembrances of Somerset Maugham. Crystal-clear waters lap against a narrow beach of white sand, and behind the beach are thick growths of sea grape and palm trees surrounding a few ramshackle but picturesque buildings. There is ample neighborly help for the passengers loaded with groceries and other supplies and friendly advice for strangers needing transportation to where they want to go. But it is all slow and casual and pleasing, even when the visitor finds that a helpful St. Johnian has put his luggage in the wrong jeep-taxi. (The driver will nearly always find out where it was supposed to go and deliver it.)

The trip to Caneel Bay Plantation is, of course, just as scenic as the public ferry ride to Cruz Bay, and over the same gorgeous stretch of water. But the attention guests embarking at the Park Service dock receive from the crew of the *Calypso* or the other Caneel boats is what it must have been like for vacationers in the 1880s at the Grand Central depot at Saratoga Springs shifting from the train into carriages on their way to spend the season at the Grand Union. Luggage disappears quickly below deck, not to be seen again until the guest walks into his airy, beach-side room on St. John; the list of passengers is checked, and with due deference everyone is escorted aboard; the gangplank is secured, and the

Lysol-clean cruiser begins its quick passage to Caneel Bay. There, on the "plantation" dock, the white faces of the hotel management smilingly greet newcomers, as small boats with striped sails dart about on the dock's off-side. Here, too, the water is amazingly clear, and there are small fish in it, but there are few pelicans. Those rather messy birds are said to be "discouraged" by the hotel management. Behind a stunning stretch of pristine white sand and a thick growth of judiciously cropped sea grape and cultivated palm trees lie, half-hidden, the cottages and buildings of the hotel. Even before the guest puts his foot on the dock, he is convinced that the $125 a day he and his wife will be spending for their accomodations will be worth it.

*   *   *

The National Park Service hands out a leaflet about the Virgin Islands National Park that says that, "St. John, smallest and least populated of the American Virgin Islands, is the one most likely to keep its virgin look." There is no doubting the Park Service's statement, for two thirds of the island's nineteen square miles are part of the National Parks system—inviolate, it is hoped, as long as we all shall live.

The park area *is* primitively wonderful and unspoiled, and on most days fairly empty. It is like Yosemite and the Grand Canyon in the days before the automobile opened them to millions of tourists, and perhaps even a little bit as this island was in the doldrum years between the great slave uprising of the early eighteenth century and the brief revival of a sugar economy in the middle nineteenth century. The Park Service has put in decent roads, much, much, better than anything on the part of the island administered by the government of the Virgin Islands, and they lead through jungly areas of second- and third-growth vegetation, fragrant with the blossoms of flowering trees. Ruins of old plantation houses and buildings are everywhere, left undisturbed because once any attempt is made to clear away the lush growths that cover them they fall apart. If the traveler is lucky, he might pick up a ride with a cruising park ranger and have a chance for an informed look at the Annaberg ruins or what is left of Frederikdal or other practically unknown places where vines and cactus grow on volcanic rock walls that some Dane or Dutchman had his slaves erect two hundred or more years ago. (Some of the ruins, it should be added, date only from the late nineteenth century, but, thanks to the instant antiquing of the tropics, even these look as if they were built in the days of Governor Lorentz.)

Traveling through the park area that encompasses nearly all of the northern and central parts of the island, one wonders how this rugged land could ever have been cultivated, for the hills are high and steep—ranging up to 1,277 feet at Bordeaux Mountain—and the work of terracing must have been horrendously difficult. No trace of the terracing remains, and, except for the ruins of great houses and roadside walls, there is little evidence of the once-flourishing plantations that covered most of the island. After a while, it is easy to leave the somewhat depressing, abandoned, overgrown hillsides for the park's beaches: Hawksnest, Trunk, Cinnamon, Maho, and Francis bays, white stretches of sand with sparkling water offshore, protected by reefs from the sweep of the North Atlantic, shallow enough for some of the finest snorkeling in the Americas but deep enough for a yachtsman to find anchorage in sea so clear that the sandy bottom seems just below the keel.

All of this unspoiled land and water—more than nine thousand acres—came under the control of the U.S. government in 1956, most of it as a gift from Laurance Rockefeller. The land surrounds the exclusive Caneel Bay Plantation resort, which the Rockefellers' Jackson Hole Foundation started after World War II. Laurance Rockefeller first become interested in buying land on St. John in its poorhouse days, about

1939, but the war intervened before he was able to acquire sizable amounts of real estate. After the war, his agents began buying in earnest and at then bargain prices. Caneel by the middle 1950s had become a "get-away-from-it-all" kind of place where a very few of the well-connected rich could relax in surroundings of expensive simplicity, not unreminiscent of the well-run camps many of them had gone to as youngsters. (Since then, Caneel has enlarged its capacity considerably and necessarily broadened its clientele; its original posh status has passed to another Rockefeller development, Little Dix Bay in the neighboring British Virgins.)

The dreadfully poor people of St. John looked on the Rockefellers coming to their island with considerable enthusiasm, and most of them welcomed the park idea. But they didn't know all of what was in the wind.

Before the National Park could be established, the Virgin Islands legislature had to give its permission. Its member from St. John, Julius Sprauve, from an old native family, eagerly introduced the necessary bill. It was quickly passed and the Department of the Interior began buying additional land to fill in areas that Laurance Rockefeller had not acquired. Most of the former owners, both those who had sold land outside the Caneel area to Rockefeller and those who later sold to the Department of the Interior, were, by the terms of their sale agreements, allowed to remain on their land for their lifetime. However, no one bothered to tell them about the new rule book they would have to follow as householders in the National Park. For generations, these natives had been freely setting fish traps and seines, cutting down trees to burn for charcoal or to build boats or repair their houses, grazing goats and cattle, gathering salt, and using the land and the adjoining waters much as they wanted to. When the U.S. Park Service rangers came in their stiff-brimmed straw hats and neat uniforms and said, "You can't do that any more," there were murmurings of revolt against Washington's long arm of the law. But except for some surreptitious fish trapping and wood cutting, nothing much happened. And Caneel Bay Plantation grew and grew within its enclave separated from the rest of raffish St. John by the *cordon sanitaire* of the Virgin Islands National Park.

The manicured resort enclave is situated on a prime stretch of the island. Besides Caneel Bay, it includes Scott Beach, Turtle Bay, Hawksnest Point, and the west shore of magnificent Hawksnest Bay. There are three private homes on the farther shore of Hawksnest Bay, but they are hidden by trees and tropical foliage and invisible to the guests in Caneel's Hawksnest section of cottages and private beach. The resort has a total of 130 guest rooms, some of them in cottages and some in two-story buildings scattered over a wide area, plus a house reserved for the use of the Laurance Rockefeller family or private guests. All are simple, but very comfortable, all unobtrusive, all close to the white sand and pellucid water in quietly preserved privacy.

Caneel is no swinging place. St. Johnians say that the guests who come to the resort are "the newly wed and the nearly dead," and there is, perhaps, a bit of truth in their joke. But, first of all, Caneel is a place for people with plenty of money to spend. During the peak December-April season, charges for single occupancy, American plan, run from $90 to $105 a day, and $110 to $115 double. A 12 per cent service charge is added, and there are additional charges for the use of snorkeling equipment, small sailboats, and bicycles, for trips on Caneel's own island schooner and sailing yacht to nearby waters, and for jeep tours of the park. Meals, served in an open-sided dining hall (buffet style for breakfast and lunch, but with plenty of black waiters from Antigua, Nevis, and other "down" islands in polite attendance even then) are bounteous if uninspired—and, of course, included in room charges. Drinks are not—and drink prices, despite duty-free liquor, are comparable to those charged in

Florida hotels. A reasonably convivial week for two people can easily cost more than $1,000—not including transportation from the mainland.

Besides well-to-do private citizens, Caneel in recent years has attracted many politicos and their families. President and Mrs. Nixon, temporarily forsaking Key Biscayne, spent a weekend there in January, 1971. Mrs. Lyndon B. Johnson has been a repeat visitor, and Patrick and Luci Johnson Nugent chose Caneel for their honeymoon. Senator Hubert H. Humphrey is a frequent guest at Caneel or Little Dix, and Mrs. Humphrey, as noted earlier, is a member of the board of directors.

Caneel Bay Plantation is run by Rockresorts, a managing agency which also operates the Rockefeller-held hideaway at Jackson Hole, Wyoming, the luxury hotel on Maui in the Hawaiian Islands, and other high-priced hostelries. Despite all the Rockefeller money available for its original development and present (profit-making) management, Caneel takes advantage of income tax write-offs and other privileges of the Virgin Islands Industrial Incentive Program.

A decade ago, when the National Park Service came very close to acquiring control of most of the rest of privately held St. John, a lot of St. Johnians came to the conclusion that Laurance Rockefeller was taking advantage of more than the Industrial Incentive Program. They decided he was taking advantage of them, too. Sabra Holbrook, a writer who lives on St. John, in her book *The American West Indies*, describes how the island's 959 residents learned what was happening:

At six o'clock on the morning of September 1, 1962, George Simmons, the government administrator of St. John, tuned his radio as usual to an English-speaking station in Puerto Rico and waited for the news. What he heard he could hardly believe. The commentator insisted that the House of Representatives of the United States Congress was about to authorize the National Park Service to acquire by *condemnation* another third of St. John. The condemnation would let the park take not all, but almost all the usable land on the island.

This legislation, which had the title "An Act to revise the boundaries of the Virgin Islands National Park, St. John, V.I.," and proposed an expansion of 5,600 acres, had originated in the Senate *nearly a year earlier*. Its stated purpose was "to preserve for the benefit of the public significant coral gardens, marine life, and seascapes in the vicinity [of the existing park]"—a laudable aim. However, besides acquiring shallow waters offshore and submerged land already owned by the federal government to protect the reefs, fish, and other sealife from human predators by extending the park generally a half mile into the sea, the bill also provided for the addition, as the larger part of the new acreage, of privately owned land, much of which was as far away from coral gardens and marine life as it is possible to get on a small island. This surprising and for months unreported action was made possible by a single sentence reading:

Within the boundaries of the Virgin Islands National Park as established and adjusted pursuant to the Act of August 2, 1956, and as revised by the Act, the Secretary of the Interior is authorized to acquire lands, waters, and interests therein by purchase, exchange, *condemnation,* or donation or with donated funds [italics added].

On September 1, 1962, the bill had already passed all of the legislative processes of the Senate. In addition, it had Department of the Interior support, as shown by a letter from Assistant Secretary of the Interior John A. Carver, dated April 13, 1962. The letter was included in the official report of the bill made to the Senate by Senator Clinton Anderson of New Mexico, its originator, on June, 1962. Carver, the man who brought the message to Ralph Paiewonsky's inauguration that the New Frontier would not "administer" the Virgin Islands, strongly backed the measure. His letter described the bill's value for the protection of spiny lobsters, coral gardens, and "brilliant tropical fish." It also said:

> We are anxious to prevent the destruction of park values on the inholdings [private lands within the proposed boundaries]. These values include tropical forests, scenic mountains, and quiet coves, all needed for full realization of the park's potential. Authority is needed whereby these lands within the boundary may be acquired by condemnation at their fair market value as soon as possible.

The bill had been scheduled for a vote in the House Rules Committee. If the committee had passed it unanimously, it would then have been voted on by the House as a whole without debate. But one member of the committee, Jack Westland of the state of Washington, asked if the people of St. John had been consulted. None of the members of the committee or its staff knew, so Westland had refused to go along with unanimous approval of the bill.

Press coverage of the complexities of congressional operation is very poor; hundreds of measures go through without attracting the attention of anyone other than careful readers of the *Congressional Record,* who are mighty few, and they mostly wear their own blinders. Committee actions are even less "newsworthy" and, unless there is some conflict, go virtually unnoticed except by bureaucrats directly concerned. However, Westland's objection did bring the bill to the attention of the Washington correspondent of the San Juan *Star,* which has a sizable circulation in the Virgin Islands. It was his wired report, used on the air, that George Simmons heard on the morning of September 1.

The residents of St. John—black natives and white continentals alike—reacted with the fury of the island's slaves during the 1733 revolt (a revolt, ironically, in which surviving white planters and their families took shelter on the estate of Peter Durlieu, now the Caneel Bay Plantation, where the rebuilt ruins of Durlieu's mill are used by the resort for cocktail parties to welcome new guests). But this new St. John revolt was peaceful, if angry.

The shaken residents did not have much time. The bill was scheduled for debate in the House in eighteen days. Sabra Holbrook describes what happened:

> Could they [the St. Johnians], in eighteen days, rally enough support to save their land? They organized a league, raised $165 to defray expenses, and set out to persuade Laurance Rockefeller to withdraw his $1.25 million and to persuade Congress to delete the condemnation clause.
>
> Within three days from the morning the news broke, two hundred St. Johnians had signed a petition, which Senator Theovald Moorehead sent to the President of the United States and to Wayne Aspinall, the Chairman of the House Committee on Interior and Insular Affairs. "We are a defenseless people without representation in Congress," the Senator's accompanying letter read "therefore we are making a last ditch appeal to your human understanding."

The islanders adopted a slogan: "No Condemnation without Representation." Soon jeep bumpers, store windows, trees, and walls were blazoned with it. By letter, telegram, and telephone, people on the mainland who had any connection with St. John were entreated to carry the islanders' plight to their congressmen. In a few days, thirty members of the House had been persuaded to vote against the bill. Former Senator Julius Sprauve, who in 1956 had introduced the bill in the Virgin Islands legislature approving establishment of the park, wrote to Representative J. T. Rutherford of Texas, chairman of the Subcommittee on National Parks:

> I would never have introduced the bill and my friends and colleagues would never have approved it without insisting that condemnation be eliminated as a firm promise forever. This

was agreed to by all parties, including Mr. Rockefeller. I consider the recent contrary actions a serious breach of faith and contract.

These islands are our home. We share their beauty gladly. But they are our only happy heritage from an unhappy past. Land ownership is tangible proof of our changed condition. Why should the homes and heritage of nearly a thousand people of St. John be sacrificed for the brief gratification of short-time park visitors who have their own safe homes to return to on the mainland?

We too are "natural objects," as park signs say. We merit at least equal protection as such.

Sprauve said he was "particularly grieved" by Laurance Rockefeller's offer of matching $1.25 million to pay for land obtained by condemnation, and he raised the bothersome issue of the exclusiveness involved, saying: "I cannot understand the distortions in human thinking that make such philanthropy somehow expressive of the love of man. It comes hard at my age to learn that St. John has been made the victim of a powerful financial and bureaucratic team-up with a different morality than our own."

Texas Congressman Rutherford, with a lawyer from Rockefeller's staff, flew to the Virgins, where the two met with Senator Theovald Moorehead, Sprauve, and other leaders of the protest movement. Rutherford went back to Washington promising to offer an amendment to the bill to remove the condemnation provision. But the St. Johnians did not relax their vigilance. Senator Moorehead went to Washington and began the task of walking the hallways of the House office buildings trying to buttonhole congressmen. A seventyish grandmother, Ethel McCully, also went to Washington, where she managed to get desk space in the office of then-Representative John V. Lindsay to carry on lobbying activities. Mrs. McCully, a retired mystery-story writer who first came to St. John in the early 1950s, was someone to be reckoned with. On board an interisland boat bound for the British Virgins, she had spotted a point of land on St. John that appealed to her as a home site and, since the boat was not cleared for landing, had jumped overboard and swum ashore to explore it. Later, she built a house there, reachable only by foot or donkey-back, in which she still lives—alone and vigorous in her eighties.*

The degree to which the residents of St. John, native and continental, organized behind the tiny island's amateur lobbyists was demonstrated by the continuous barrage laid down on Congress, many of whose members in 1956 knew so little of the Virgin Islands that some thought they were called the "Virginia Islands." The surprised congressmen got maps of the islands and asked for copies of the treaty between Denmark and the United States that guaranteed to "protect the peaceful possession of property by private individuals." Representative Aspinall, who ran his Interior and Insular Affairs Committee like a private club, was bombarded with telegrams—seven hundred of them from a place with a population of less than one thousand. Despite the telegrams, when the bill came up for debate on September 18, crusty Wayne Aspinall made a long speech in favor of it. But he was shamming. Toward the end of his disquisition on the benefits of expanding the park, he announced that Laurance Rockefeller no longer wanted condemnation. It might have been more accurate to say that Rockefeller had decided that the proposal had caused too much trouble and had withdrawn his matching $1.25 million. Representative Rutherford offered his amendment deleting the word "condemnation," which was accepted, and the bill eventually was passed, but without authorization for the appropriation of government

---

* When I first heard of Mrs. McCully's use of Lindsay's office and saw a picture of her taken with him at the time, it crossed my mind that this episode might have represented his first brush with the Rockefeller clan. If so, his protective present staff deny it. They say he has no recollection of it.

funds. The 959 St. Johnians had won a famous victory. When Representative Westland, whose question had fortuitously triggered their resistance to further inroads on their property in the name of conservation, visited the island in late 1962, Sabra Holbrook says, "The people gave him a steel band party in the village square unequalled even by their annual Fourth of July celebrations."

The Virgin Islands National Park has since extended its boundaries seaward, achieving what was stated in the 1962 Act as its basic (and clearly legal and proper) purpose. Indiscriminate chopping of coral from the reefs for souvenirs, destructive spearfishing and water skiing, and hotrodding in outboard motorboats, which endangers swimmers and snorkelers, have been stopped. A little additional land volunteered for sale has been acquired for the park by the Department of the Interior with special funds that now and then have become available. But the people of St. John retain their treaty right to hold their land as they see fit.

The big question of what Julius Sprauve called "morality" remains. Why should Laurance Rockefeller, sitting in his office at 30 Rockefeller Plaza, have the power, denied to him in this instance only by a fluke of Capitol Hill reportage, to use the democratic processes of the U.S. legislature to take over other people's homes, however environmentally protective and philanthropic his motives? (Ethel McCully says that she believes Rockefeller was not fully aware of what had been going on. "I think," she told me, "the matter was handled by people on his staff." It is possibly true that Rockefeller can afford to authorize employees to hand out $1.25 million without being aware of what the money is buying.) Particularly disturbing is Congress's nearly automatic reaction to the Rockefeller offer, without even bothering to send a committee staff assistant to look into the situation. And even more disturbing is the eager support given to the project by Assistant Secretary Carver, under whose jurisdiction the Office of Territories and hence the Virgin Islands came, without so much as sounding out St. Johnian opinion.

In October, 1971, I wrote to John J. Kirwan, who was acting director of Interior's Office of Territories in 1962, asking him about Interior's rationale at the time the land condemnation was proposed. "With regard to the St. John Park matter, I have no recollection of it," he answered. "It is inconceivable to me that any bill of the import you describe would not have been known in all its major provisions to those people in the islands who might be expected to follow such things—e.g., the editor of the *Daily News*, the Government Secretary, the Governor, party officials, etc." "But," he wrote, "my vagueness here is largely due to National Park matters never having been a part of my responsibility."

Perhaps Governor Paiewonsky may have known something about the bill at the time, and so possibly may some of the others. But Ariel Melchior, then and now editor of the *Daily News*, said, "The first time I knew anything about what was going on was when I saw a bunch of St. Johnians coming down Main Street here in Charlotte Amalie with 'No Condemnation without Representation' signs on their hats."

It would be gratifying to report that everyone on the never-never island of St. John lived happily ever after. Such, unfortunately, has not been the case. Since the victory of 1962, the island's population has doubled, and the economic growth that has defaced St. Thomas and scarred St. Croix has spilled over to St. John. The somewhat unkempt air of the privately held part of the island, which once was an element of its charm, is giving way, here and there, to that plastic-world seediness found around small towns of the Appalachian chain from New York State to the Carolinas: trailer homes, jerry-built houses on slashed-out hillsides, abandoned automobiles, thrown-away refrigerators, and other eyesores of modern America. Up to mid-1972, the "developers" had not made much headway on the island. But the signs that some have tried are there to affront the eye and mind.

One entrepreneur blasted part of the reef protecting Great Cruz Bay at the island's southeastern corner, dredged thousands of tons of sand from the shallow water of the bay, and made a beach where before there had been a mangrove swamp. In the process, according to Doris Jadan's *Guide to the Natural History of St. John,* he created "an underwater desert," as all sealife was destroyed by silt and turbidity. He also, as the visitor can all too readily see, created desolation on the land. The dredged sand has killed the mangroves and other shore growth and, in addition, has blocked a natural drainage outlet for surface water from a large area of hills behind the bay, a blockage that during rainstorms floods the road to town used by a sizable number of people near Chocolate Hole and Rendezvous Bay. Apparently the Great Cruz developer has run short of money. To date, nothing has been done with the property.

For Chocolate Hole, so called because of the color of the rocks at its entrance, another developer has drawn up plans for a large condominium complex that looks impressive in his brochure. But to accomplish what is needed, the developer will have to do a good deal of blasting and dredging and general tearing away of the tropical vegetation that now holds soil on the steep hillsides and protects the narrow existing beach. Although in mid-1972 this project was still in the paper stage, it was worrying residents of the hills overlooking the quiet piece of water. The Virgin Islands Planning Commission has obligingly declared Great Cruz Bay and Chocolate Hole "W-1" (Waterfront-Industrial) areas for "residential, bars, restaurants, clubs, bowling alleys, etc." with a density of forty people per acre.

These typically short-sighted zoning assignments are at the opposite end of the development pole from the Rockefellercum-National Park approach to land use. Whether the residents of St. John find a firm middle ground in the large area between primitive park and clustered condominiums and can settle on the kind of island they want is still an open question. It must be hard for any native of the once all-poor Caribbean to resist a stateside operator who comes to the house waving a checkbook and talking in terms of the tens and even hundreds of thousands of dollars he will pay for the family homestead. But it is just possible that the St. Johnians may be able to turn deaf ears to the blandishments of further development—of any kind. They are a tightly knit, interdependent community of the sort that, to their mixed blessing, truly isolated islands produce. (The ferry that runs every hour from Cruz Bay to Red Hook is a relatively recent addition to the island's amenities. When Julius Sprauve was in the legislature in the mid-1950s, never missing a day in attendance, he often rowed the four miles of Pillsbury Sound to St. Thomas if there were no other boats available.)

Up to now, development has produced little change in the island's society. The small continental population, about 175 of the island's present 1,700 residents, has had to become a real part of St. Johnian life—a not too difficult adjustment since the kind of people from the mainland who have settled on St. John came exactly because of the island's isolation and simplicity, which they strongly want to preserve. Despite their small number, these relative newcomers (few have been there for more than twenty years) play an important local role. Unlike their fellow continentals on St. Thomas and St. Croix, whose attitude generally is "leave it to the natives," these people, in their shorts and tennis shoes and shifts-over-bikinis, have been vigorously working to preserve the unspoiled, birthright St. John. Moreover, most of the natives realize that the aftermath of selling their property for quick gain is living in a St. Thomian or Crucian environment, leagues removed from what they know and enjoy on

St. John, and on money that will be quickly spent. So far, more of them than not appear to prefer holding on to what they have and hewing to the not-too-bad older ways.

But what if hard times come again as they have before? Or if the youngsters prefer a different, jazzier life? Will the St. Johnians, once seduced by the National Park development and Laurance Rockefeller's millions, and the second time around strong enough to say no even to the U.S. Congress, be able in an unclear future to make it on their own? Since a seducer is also, at least for a while, a protector, and the St. Johnians, like all of us, may need protection, if only from the greedier side of their own natures, the question is freighted.

8. Politics, Calypso Style

    Lindquist's Beach on St. Thomas's north shore, a favorite spot with the island-born for group picnics, is what residents say the Virgin Islands were like twenty years ago. You reach it by a sandy track that runs about 300 yards off Red Hook Road to Smith's Bay. The facilities are rudimentary: a couple of ramshackle, unpainted buildings and a tin-roofed open dance floor of concrete shaded by a thick grove of jungly trees. Sea grape grows along the beach, here and there the twisted roots reaching to the high-tide mark. Today's beach clubs, cottages, and condominiums, with their planted palms and careful landscaping, their yacht docks and beachfront bars, seem far away. Lindquist's is old-fashioned tropics, the kind that used to be.

    In 1970, Lindquist's was also a favorite spot for all-out political picnics, the kind that the U.S. mainland once used to have. But with several differences. When I visited the beach, the place was jumping. A quarter-mile from the entrance, where I finally found a place to park in an open field crowded with old heaps and shiny new cars, jeeps, and open trucks, you could hear Milo and His Kings blasting away. In the grove, a bar was set up with a half-dozen sweating men and women behind it wearing that now-universal headgear of political campaigns, plastic boaters with red, white, and blue bands. The bands on these were emblazoned VOTE KING. I was there as a hired hand, speechwriter for the former number-two man in the Paiewonsky regime, who was now the candidate of the Independent Citizens Movement in the first gubernatorial campaign in the history of the American Virgins.

The crowd around the bar was two deep, and the bartenders had difficulty hearing, over Milo's calypso rhythms blaring from the loudspeakers, the orders for Courvoisier and Coke, Cutty and soda, and Carlsberg beer. (No one drinks plebian Seagram's 7 or Schlitz in the "duty-free" Virgin Islands.) There was a long line waiting for food at a nearby shed where a dozen women were dishing out bull-foot soup, stewed goat, kallaloo, fungi, fried yellow-tail, fried chicken, and johnny cakes. The dance floor, behind the bar, was jampacked with shoulder-shaking, sweating people of all ages, moving as only West Indians can to the heavy brass and percussion of the band. But the people on the floor were not the only ones in movement. No one in the crowd around the dance floor seemed able to keep still. Near me a mother, not young, danced with a baby in her arms. The jiggling child, feeling the beat, gurgled with delight.

When the set ended, someone yelled "Obstinate! Obstinate!" The crowd took up the cry, until a tall black with the build of a National Football League wide receiver ambled through the crowd. He was wearing a tight cerise shirt with extraordinarily long collar points, unbuttoned to the diaphragm, and tight, tight, tight yellow bell-bottoms. He took the microphone from its stand, nodded to the band, which gave him an eight-bar introduction, and started:

> The Virgin Island nex' gover-nor is need to be a giant.
> He has to be for all the people, not just a client.

The song was King Obstinate's "Ideal Governor," which the Antiguan calypso celebrity had written in the spring. For

months it had been played over and over again on the local
radio stations. The crowd loved it.

Obstinate moved with strong grace, perspiration pouring
down his face, for, as is frequent in October when the trade
winds slacken, there was no breeze.

> If there is a man, will you kindly raise your hand—
> I mean a man with a lot of wit and skill.
> For the future looks very dim,
> So let's get the best man for the job on Government Hill.

The crowd roared.

"Cyril King! Cyril King! Cyril King!"

The band started up again with a driving, repetitive introduction. Obstinate opened with the new campaign song
he had written the week before:

> Vote Cyril King.
> Vote Cyril King.
> On November third,
> King is the word.

The music was supremely simple but compelling, and the
crowd went wild. The dancing changed. Arms were thrust
into the air, jerking to the rhythm, Africa alive in the scene.
The few whites in the throng, mostly people from French-
town and Mafolie, on the outskirts of Charlotte Amalie,
were with the beat, too. Obstinate repeated the refrain three
times, put the microphone back in its stand, and left the
floor. The crowd renewed the cry, "Cyril King! Cyril King!"

Finally, a little, freckle-faced Frenchman took the microphone. "Okay. Okay. But first let me introduce the Virgin
Islands' own champion, who is for our champion, Emile
Griffith." Griffith, former welterweight and middleweight
champion of the world, came to the microphone, a big grin
on his battered black face. He said nothing, but clasped his
hands above his head in a fighter's salute.

"And now," the Frenchman intoned, "the next governor

of the Virgin Islands, Cyril King." The band broke into Obstinate's "Vote Cyril King!" again. Amid the roar of the crowd, a light-skinned black with a white poll and a thin, dark mustache walked through the lane made for him on the dance floor. His open-necked white sport shirt looked as if it had just come from the laundry, and, in contrast to the crowd, he himself had the freshness of a man who had just stepped from a cool shower. Two big men in plastic boaters picked him up and boosted him to their shoulders. For a fleeting moment, he looked annoyed as his head nearly brushed the rafters, but he quickly broke into a huge, youthful grin. Set down at the microphone, he thanked the crowd briefly, said to keep the party going, then walked to his car and drove away with his waiting wife and daughter.

The party did keep going. I left at dark, but the next morning at ICM headquarters some of the bleary-eyed organizers told me that they had had to put out the lights at ten o'clock to get the stayers-on to go home. The picnic had started at one in the afternoon. The Independent Citizens Movement had netted $1,800.

* * *

The native Virgin Islander takes to politics like the Boston Irishman of old, although perhaps with less single-mindedness. Parties like the one at Lindquist's Beach are frequent and enjoyed by all. In a Charlotte Amalie drugstore one Sunday morning I overheard two young men talking about what to do with the rest of the day. "Let's go to a picnic, mon," one said. "Whose picnic?" the other asked. "I don't care whose picnic—Democrat, ICM, Republican. I just feel like going to a picnic."

But the picnics, rallies, house parties, and other political doings that filled several months of 1970 had a new and special significance for the islanders. For sixteen years they had been voting for candidates for the legislature. Now they were about to elect the first governor of their own choosing. Congress in the summer of 1968 had passed the Virgin Islands Elective Governor Act, signed by President Johnson on August 28. Governor Paiewonsky, while the bill was in the legislative process, had tried to persuade Congress to make the law effective for the November, 1968, election so that he could be a candidate, but Paiewonsky's political star had faded—in Washington and on the islands—and the November, 1970, election date was made a part of the Act.

Campaigning for the job began almost as long before that election as the campaign for the 1972 presidential election. Cyril King was first in the field, making his announcement on December 12, 1969, at a dinner ostensibly organized as a testimonial to honor his eight and a half years as government secretary, a job he had left at the end of September. The announcement was not unexpected. Immediately after resigning as government secretary, he had taken over the leadership of the fledgling Independent Citizens Movement, a group born during the legislative campaign of 1968. Dissidents of all stripes had joined ICM, but its principal membership was made up of old Donkey Democrats who had found themselves partyless when the courts gave the Paiewonsky-Ottley organization the sole right to the title "Democrats." In the 1968 election, ICM had put together a partial slate of candidates and, to everyone's surprise, including their own, had polled 33 per cent of the vote. (The Republicans, allowed on the ballot only by legislative act because of the small number of votes they got in the 1966 elections, had polled 7 per cent.)

The Democrats paid little attention to King's announced candidacy; with 100 per cent control of the legislature, they were too busy frustrating recently appointed Republican Governor Evans's legislative efforts and too involved with intraparty maneuvering in preparation for November, 1970. Until the late spring of 1970, ICM remained the only organization with an announced candidate.

Cyril King, before being appointed by President John F. Kennedy in 1961, had worked for twelve years on the Washington staff of then-Senator Hubert H. Humphrey, a job he got after graduating from college. Even before the Paiewonsky-Ottley takeover of the Democratic label, King had begun to have serious differences with his governor, which as described, resulted in the Democratic senators' legislating away most of the government secretary's major responsibilities. With the election of President Nixon, Paiewonsky's eight-year tenure came to an end (although he hung on until he was asked to resign). The first man proposed as his successor withdrew—because, it is said, of a combination of ill health and some raised senatorial eyebrows over his qualifications. King was appointed acting governor to fill the vacancy until the White House could come up with another appointment. Despite the "acting" title, during the months he held the post—from February to July, 1969—he attacked the job as if it were permanent, killing a number of Paiewonsky's expensive projects because, he said, there were no funds, sending home a half-dozen $150-a-day consultants from the mainland, and putting pressure on the hordes of easy-going government workers to start working. These reforms won him the respect of a number of solid citizens. But they also roused the anger and enmity of the Democratic organization and its supporters, who had grown so used to untrammeled freewheeling that it seemed their birthright.

No other announced candidate appeared on the scene until June, 1970. Then, Senator Alexander Farrelly, a prosperous and aristocratic-looking black lawyer who had been an assistant U.S. attorney and municipal court judge, said he would seek the Democratic nomination. A few weeks later, another black lawyer, Francisco "Kiko" Corneiro, entered the Democratic race. Although it was not officially announced at the time, everyone knew Farrelly to be the candidate of Democratic boss Earle Ottley, while Corneiro, who had been attorney general in the Paiewonsky regime, was known to be Paiewonsky's choice. On the Republican side there was silence. Governor Evans took to parrying questions about his plans with a question of his own: "Do you think I am a candidate?" But he appeared more and more on television and radio, getting plenty of exposure from the free time that was his due to report to the people on this and that.

The first candidate to be officially nominated was King, although it took two ICM convention sessions two weeks apart to do it. Not that he had opposition. But even with his early start, King had not been able to put together a full slate of candidates. He had trouble persuading people that he had a chance of winning, and he also ran into the natural fear of many Virgin Islanders who in one way or another depended on the government for their livelihood that there would be reprisals if they bucked the powerful Democratic machine.

The first ICM convention session opened on July 10 with all the trappings of such a political meeting on the mainland: banners, placards, delegation standards, endless parliamentary rigamarole, speeches, and music (calypso style). Only a handful of spectators were on hand in the rather dingy third-story auditorium of the Charlotte Amalie Catholic high school. Although King had managed to put together a full slate of fifteen senatorial candidates, including four schoolteachers, he still needed a running mate for the lieutenant-governor's job and someone to oppose the Democratic incumbent for the job of the islands' Washington representative. After some frantic, and unsuccessful, efforts in the night to find people willing to run, the convention reconvened the following morning, adopted the platform, and recessed for two weeks.

During this period, the Virgin Islands *Daily News,* which had been all-out in support of King's candidacy, discovered that some campaign material had arrived from the mainland for Evans. A reporter got hold of some bumper stickers reading "Thank Heavens for Evans" and some cardboard placards, and, on July 16, the paper ran a story about the reporter's find. The following day, Evans went on television with a "special announcement." Yes, he would run for governor.

Governor Evans, like King, had had his troubles with the Democratic machine. A cardiologist, Dr. Evans had been assistant commissioner of health for the island of St. Croix from 1951 to 1955 and commissioner of health for the territory from 1955 into the latter Paiewonsky years. He was then a Democrat. In 1966, the Paiewonsky regime put up $20,000 to allow him a "sabbatical year" to study public health at the University of California at Berkeley, but when he got back to St. Thomas, he found that the islands' Democratic National Committeeman had been given his job on a permanent basis. He turned down a sinecure at his commissioner's pay and returned to his home island of St. Croix to go into private practice. There, in September, 1968, two months before President Nixon nosed out Senator Humphrey, he changed his registration to Republican, opening the way for his selection (second choice) as the last appointed governor of the Virgin Islands. (The first choice was a man named Peter Bove, a white continental who had preceded Ross as government comptroller. Before coming to the Virgins on an appointment by the Eisenhower Administration, he had been a liquor administrator in Vermont.)

On July 25, the Independent Citizens Movement reconvened its convention. During the recess, King had managed to persuade a veteran government official, Hugh M. Smith, a former Virgin Islands champion in golf and tennis, to run with him as candidate for lieutenant-governor and a relatively unknown woman lawyer, Mrs. Lucia Galiber, the wife of a St. Croix dentist, to run for the position of Washington representative. The nominations were a mere formality.

While ICM was reconvening on St. Thomas, the Democrats were holding their convention on St. Croix with a packed house, confident speechmaking, floodlights, and the cameras of the St. Croix and St. Thomas television stations covering the affair. Paiewonsky's Corneiro, with only five votes, never had a chance against the Ottley machine. The Democratic Party had Alexander Farrelly as its candidate, a choice that many rank-and-file members had difficulty swallowing because they felt that he was "too snooty."

The Republicans also convened on St. Croix to put the party stamp on their candidate, Governor Evans. Evans had none of the trouble King did in finding a running mate; his was ready-made—the incumbent government secretary, David E. Maas, a fifty-six-year-old white, former FBI man, lawyer, and one-time owner of the cottages and condominiums at expensive Sapphire Beach on St. Thomas. Maas, a registered Republican from the time he came to the islands in 1945, had been mentioned as a possible successor to Ralph Paiewonsky when Nixon was elected. He was the only white at the top of the ticket in the three parties.

A week after the Democratic convention chose Farrelly, and after conferring with Ralph Paiewonsky, "Kiko" Corneiro announced that he would oppose the convention's choice, making a primary election necessary. As the Ottley-Farrelly and Paiewonsky-Corneiro forces battled among themselves, filling the airways with radio and television spots, plastering the islands with placards and stickers, serving out free food and booze at beach parties, and making the day and night bedlam with touring sound trucks, activity in the Republican and ICM camps slowed perceptibly. During this period, however, Governor Evans was very busy officially, cutting ribbons, handing out awards, inspecting building projects, and generally making himself visible. The Republican National Committee sent him a savvy semi-retired black, Gene Washington, who for many years had been one of its advisers on racial problems, and the Evans people also added two public relations men from the mainland to the governor's official staff. ICM candidate King occupied himself principally with ringing doorbells and attending house parties in the white community, where he felt himself to be weak. (The white continentals, old and new, were seldom to be seen at any of the public political functions during the campaign.) He also continued a series of television talks that he had started before the ICM convention had nominated him. His professional staff, besides myself (an Irish mercenary recommended to ICM by friends on the Democratic Study Group in Congress), consisted of Jimmy Jones, a veteran black assistant to I. W. Abell, president of the United Steel Workers Union, whose job was to whip the precinct workers into line (which he did with all the zeal of an old-fashioned union organizer), and a white candidate for the senate, Ed Moran, who had been King's assistant when he was acting governor.

The primary election to choose the Democratic candidate was held on September 8. Despite a party registration of more than 14,000 and the urging of the bosses, only a few more than 7,000 went to the polls—not even the total number of government employees. As everyone expected, Farrelly won. But he won by a scant 300 votes. The hold of the Ottley-run Democratic machine had been found to be less than absolute. As is usual after a primary, the victorious faction went to the loser to solicit his support. Surprisingly, Corneiro turned stubborn. He would support Farrelly, he said, only if Farrelly would disown the machine. When Farrelly would not, Corneiro remained silent, and kept silent through the elections to come.

* * *

Elections in the Virgin Islands are taken very seriously. Voter participation averages about 20 per cent higher than on the mainland during presidential years. The elections can be rough affairs. In his book *The U.S. Virgins and the Eastern Caribbean,* Darwin Creque, a native islander, told what it was like about a decade ago:

The audience expected mudslinging and they got it. Candidates thought it was their civic duty to expose the social background of their opponents and showed no mercy for those unfortunate enough to have been born out of wedlock, or for those whose parents had served a jail term for borrowing without the consent of the victim. The audience usually listened intently. If they liked the candidate's speech, he was roundly applauded and was permitted to leave the rostrum unmolested. If, on the other hand, the audience disliked the candidate's speech or had misgivings about his allegations, he was pelted with stones and driven off the rostrum, despite the presence of the law.

Then there were those who indulged in character assassination. During a political campaign in St. Croix a candidate called his opponent, who was absent from the scene, an "alley cat." The crowd roared. The following week, his rival took to the rostrum and lampooned his cunning adversary by calling him a "sewer rat" who had to be destroyed by the "alley cat" for the preservation of health. This evened the score. On election day, however, the "alley cat" was victorious at the polls, winning by a whisker.

The 1970 campaign did not reach such heights. No stones were thrown, and there were no direct accusations of felony or bastardy, although there were whispers about the ancestry of some of the lesser candidates. All the same, it was a lively time.

The methods of the three candidates were so different that it might have been thought they were running for different jobs. Evans stood above the battle, poised on his "accomplishments," and appearing frequently on television—a medium that showed him to considerable advantage as a kindly, straight-talking family-doctor type. What criticism he expressed was directed at the Democratic legislature, which he accused of preventing him from carrying out his "progressive" programs. Farrelly said little and appeared less, in public or on the radio or television, depending on canned radio and television commercials and on the other candidates to sell the ticket. Neither the Republicans nor the Democrats paid much attention to the ICM candidate, although King's earnest and angry campaigning attacked them both. King had dug deeply into Comptroller Howard Ross's 1969 report of the peccadilloes and shortcomings of the Paiewonsky regime and played them back to the electorate with embellishments. He also tried to tie Evans to the shortcomings of the Nixon administration in Washington and, taking a word from the civil rights vocabulary, accused him of "tokenism" in his approach to government.

The three more-or-less daily newspapers on the islands split three ways in their editorial support. The St. Croix *Avis* backed Evans, but with some objectivity. The *Daily News* of Charlotte Amalie was all out for King, although it did report on the doings of the other candidates. Earle Ottley's *Home Journal,* also on St. Thomas, of course was for Farrelly, but so one-sidely that King's headquarters did not even bother to send it press releases.

Campaign financing for the Republicans and the Democrats was no problem. Evans's people, with control of Government House and the governor's large staff, and with recourse to the Republican National Committee in Washington, had little trouble finding money for radio and television, posters, bumper stickers, buttons, hats, sound trucks, and all the other paraphernalia of today's political campaigning. The Democrats, with years of unchallenged control of the Virgin Islands' purse behind them and more than seven thousand government workers to do their bidding, were even better off financially than the Republicans. King ran a poor man's campaign, although he had numerous silent contributors, including some in Washington, and always seemed to find money when money was needed. (Throughout the pre-election period, he acted as his own treasurer—and campaign manager—and no one, excepting his accountant, ever knew what funds were available at a given moment.) One indication of the relative financial positions of the three candidates was that Republican and Democratic beach parties were all free-loading affairs; those held by ICM were fund-raisers.

A major election issue emerged coincidentally with the Democratic primary, which came at the same time as the scheduled opening of the public schools. On September 9, the day when all students were supposed to return to classes, only those in the first three grades were accepted. Governor Evans's administration had not yet figured out what to do with all the new pupils—nearly 20 per cent more of them than the fifteen thousand enrolled the year before. Slightly more than half of this increase was due to a U.S. District Court order in July that required the admission of previously excluded children of bonded aliens, who until 1970 had been allowed to work in the Virgin Islands and pay income taxes into the island government's coffers but could not send their children to the tax-supported schools. Even if the aliens had not been added to the Department of Education's problems there would not have been enough room for all of the citizens' children: Three schools that were supposed to have been ready for the 1970 school year were far from being completed, and twenty-six trailers, ordered only four weeks earlier, to be used as "relocatable classrooms," had not yet arrived from the supplier in Pennsylvania.

King made a tour of the schools on St. Thomas on the scheduled opening day, and then went on television indignantly charging that the situation was "chaotic," as indeed it was. The following week, after all of the schools and all grades were officially opened, he went to St. Croix, where he found, among others things, the 1,400 students at the Central High School milling about the area with no classes in session. The principal was at a meeting in Christiansted, five miles away. A combined elementary and junior high school in Christiansted had two cooks in the kitchen to prepare lunch for nearly 2,500 students. King went on television again to describe what he had seen, and in the same week, the Farrelly forces, taking a leaf from ICM's book, made tours of the schools and broadcast similar findings on radio and television.

The bipartisan needles apparently hurt Governor Evans. On his weekly television broadcast, for the first time he tore into King and Farrelly attacking them for interfering with school affairs and likening them, curiously, to "the citizens councils who obstructed integration in the schools of the South."

Until this odd moment, the election campaign, to all public intents and purposes, might have been going on in rural Iowa so far as racial matters were concerned, although a whispering campaign had begun in the white community—particularly on St. Croix—that King was a "black power advocate." This tag, incongruous in a place where blacks had dominated political affairs for so long, sat strangely with Evans's direct attack on King, who, he said, had acted "like George Wallace, standing in the schoolhouse door." Then Farrelly's running mate, Elmo Roebuck, pointed out in a radio speech that the election of Evans, with Maas as his running mate, would "put a white man a heartbeat away from the governor's chair," a statement frequently repeated as the weeks went by. The campaign was beginning to heat up and, it might be said, to take on color.

In October, under the prodding of the Ottley organization, Farrelly became more active and announced that he would deliver a series of speeches, which he called "white papers," describing the programs he would carry out as governor. He delivered three, saying little more than that he would pursue programs begun during the Paiewonsky administration. Next, Ralph Paiewonsky himself took to television for a "series of broadcasts" paid for out of his well-filled pocket. The series began with, and never went beyond, one thirty-minute celebration of his eight years in Government House. The Democrats seemed to be in disorder. Their "snooty" candidate, a Yale Master of Law, obviously was not getting through to the voters in the backstreets of Charlotte Amalie, Frederiksted, and Christiansted, and the crowded new developments in which many of the poor and the lower middle class had been forced to settle. A boost came from Washington, duly announced by advertisements in all the newspapers, on radio, and on television, in the form of an endorsement by Senator Edward M. Kennedy of his fellow-Democrat Farrelly. (No one at the time bothered to check with Washington to see how this endorsement came about, but aides of Senator Kennedy said long after the election that it was "just routine" and a "post-primary thing we do all the time for party candidates." Neither Senator Kennedy himself nor anyone in his office knew Farrelly. Presumably, they also knew little or nothing of the operators who were his supporters.)

Despite the Kennedy support, the Democratic organization apparently felt the election to be slipping away from them and persuaded the gentlemanly Farrelly to take the offensive. One weekend in mid-October, the airwaves suddenly were filled with spot announcements every ten minutes or so that Senator Farrelly would "make his most important speech of the campaign" on radio and television the following Sunday afternoon. Completely ignoring Republican Governor Evans, Farrelly went after King, whom he characterized as "inexperienced in the ways of government," a "mere clerk" in Senator Humphrey's office, a man "without the training and ability" to hold the office of governor. He then spent the rest of his speech describing his own educational background, legal training, "judicial" experience (although his job on the municipal court had been limited to small claims and arraignments of people arrested by the police), and his service in the Virgin Islands legislature. King reacted and, ticking off the various governmental positions he had held, accused Farrelly of "losing his Ivy League cool." Governor Evans in Government House kept quiet, undoubtedly enjoying the hassle between his two rivals, both of whom he knew well from the days—not too long before—when they had all been Democrats together.

On election day, November 3, it rained—hard. The voter turnout was tremendous nevertheless. Some 80 per cent of the 18,500 registered went to the polls. When the votes were counted in the early morning of November 4, King, to the surprise of many, was on top with 5,422 ballots; Evans was second with 4,926; and Farrelly last with 4,634. As the Elective Governor Act required the winner to have "fifty percent of the votes plus one," a runoff between King and Evans was required, so the end was not yet. But something astonishing had happened.

The voters of the American Virgins had not only rejected the entrenched machine Democrats' gubernatorial candidate by more than two to one but also had shattered the Democratic Party's absolute control of the legislature. Only four of the old Ottley gang, including Earle Ottley himself, were re-elected. The Democrats picked up two other seats with the election of two young, first-time candidates, the manager of the islands' only all-black radio station and a young black Christiansted businessman, the latter the party's only winner on St. Croix. But King's ICM also elected six senators. One of them, Alexander A. Moorhead, Jr., a twenty-five-year-old who had been a "Little All-American" in basketball at Moravian College in Bethlehem, Pennsylvania, ran ahead of all of the candidates for all offices. For a senator-at-large seat he polled 5,721 votes, 299 more than King himself. The Republicans, as had been expected, showed considerable strength on St. Croix, winning three of that island's six senatorial contests.

* * *

By law the runoff was set for November 17. Hardly had the November 3 votes been counted when Earle Ottley and some other Democrats got together in a St. Thomas hotel with some Republicans, including Governor Evans and his white running-mate, David Maas (who had been almost invisible during the campaign). Although only days before Evans had been saying that the Democrats were "corrupt," "undemocratic," and "obstructive," and the Democrats had been tarring him, in mainland fashion, with the worn-out brush of Herbert Hooverism, the meeting apparently went well, for in a few days the Republicans and the Democrats were working as one. The *Daily News* screamed "Deal!" and its publisher, Ariel Melchior, Sr., whose son had won an ICM senate seat, produced an eight-page handout for King, dubbing the new coalition "Republocrats." In the handout's pages the rhetoric of earlier years was resurrected. One disaffected Democrat wrote in it:

> How these people can have the bravura to turn about face on their own previous denouncements of the Republicans is a remarkable display of Democratic senility from which they and they alone are suffering. They must suddenly have developed cataracts over their eyes. And their tongues seem to have turned upside down in their palates. . . . Skunks have never inhabited the Virgin Islands but in the last few days there has been a noticeable skunk odor around, and we don't like it.

In the same handout there appeared a bitter piece under the headline "The True Melvin Evans" by Esther Moorhead, mother of the Senator-elect Moorhead.

Let us examine Governor Evans' life from the time he returned to these islands as a doctor in Frederiksted. Since his mother who worked in a grocery store to put him through school lived in Christiansted and his only relative in Frederiksted was not living a Christian life, he had to turn to friends to take him in until he could get on his feet. Mrs. Esther Moorhead . . . threw open her doors to him. . . . Uncle Melvin, as the children affectionately called him, was one of the family.

At the end of two months, Uncle Melvin decided he was well in the black (he was the only doctor in Frederiksted) and he wanted to contribute a little toward his keep. Beginning at the end of the following month until he got married and moved into his own place, he gave [the Moorheads] $30 each month, $1 a day, for his meals and room. That could have been reason for Governor Evans' saying at the Frederiksted Civic Association banquet last year that his first landlord was Mr. Schade. He paid real rent there and bought his own groceries.

Mrs. Moorhead's article went on to tell how relations cooled when her daughter married Melvin H. Evans, Jr., who "left his bride a few hours after the ceremony and has never been allowed to return," and how "Uncle Melvin" —as she put it—"had federal marshals, rifles, and sub-machine guns brought in" when Mario Moorhead, another of her sons, was arrested. "This man," she wrote, "has used his friends to push him up where he would like to go. After he gets there he forgets you are alive. This Christian has forgotten that the good book says, 'Vengeance is mine. I will repay.' "

Whether this kind of old-fashioned rhetoric, riddled with primitive hatred, had a plus or minus effect on voters between the two election days is hard to determine. But emotionalism was by no means confined to King's supporters. The undercover charges that King was a "black power advocate" now came into the open, as Evans himself termed King a "racist"—a word that in the white and conservative-black lexicon of the Virgin Islands meant "anti-establishment," but one that rang discordantly in the black society of the territory. In my view, the King people handled the charges poorly. During the campaign, King had been calm and circumspect about "black power," answering the charge when it occasionally surfaced in questions put to him by saying that of course he was black, and since the vast majority of the Virgin Islanders also were black, they should have the power to control their political system. But between the election days, two of King's more ardent young supporters went on the radio, one to revive again the Democrats' warning that the election of Evans running mate, Maas, would put "a white man a heartbeat away from the governor's chair," and the other to emphasize the need for Virgin Islanders to elect a ticket that was "culturally" of the islands. Among the new whites on the islands, particularly on St. Croix, these speeches did not go down well.

King also alienated some of the more sophisticated islanders, blacks and continentals, when he refused to talk to a reporter from the San Juan *Star*, a Puerto Rican newspaper with a circulation of several thousand on the islands. Like many people unused to talking to metropolitan newspapermen, King, as acting governor, had been burned twice, first by a wire-service reporter and then by a reporter for the New York *Times*, to both of whom he had talked freely, only to be appalled when he saw his words in print. The San Juan *Star* ran an interview with Governor Evans, and the managing editor of the paper telephoned King from San Juan to urge him, too, to talk to his reporter. But King's antipathy to outside newspapermen was too great. He refused, and the following morning the paper ran an editorial that understandably wondered what kind of a governor King would be if he were not willing to talk to the press.

Meanwhile, the Democrats were busy all over the islands spreading the word that King, if elected, would "swing a meat-axe" in all government departments. King indignantly denied any such intention, but everyone knew that he would have to do just that if he wanted to put into effect the kind of government he had been talking about since December, 1969.

High-powered outside support arranged for King by friends in Washington helped him to redress the balance somewhat. Hubert Humphrey, who had just been re-elected to the Senate, did three television spots supporting his former staffer, which ICM used extensively on the stations in St. Thomas and St. Croix. Fourteen members of Congress—all Democrats, and among them Shirley Chisholm, of New York, and John Conyers, of Michigan, both black, and Herman Badillo, of New York, the first Puerto Rican to be elected to Congress—signed a published statement supporting King's candidacy. But these last-minute assists from the liberal Democrats of Washington proved to be insufficient.

On November 17, the runoff day, more than two thirds of the Evans workers at the polls were from the Ottley machine, people who knew the voters and were expert at doing the things that experienced political workers do at the polls to influence votes. The turnout was even larger than it had been on November 3, with nearly 16,000 voting. When the count began that night, the effectiveness of the "Republocrats" last-minute organization quickly became evident. In the places where Alexander Farrelly had shown some strength on November 3, the vote had shifted to Evans. On St. Croix, where the Republicans had done well the first time, Evans ran ahead of King.

Before midnight, the result was certain: Evans had been elected. When all the votes were counted, the margin turned out to be relatively small, but decisive—Evans got 8,259 and King 7,452. The Virgin Islands had its first elected governor, a Republican—who, since the legislature was split, would have to make further postelection accomodations with the Democrats to get some kind of working majority. The new governor, it was immediately clear, had his problems.

There also remained at nightfall on November 17 the

underlying political and human problem that no one had had the courage to talk about during the long months of speechmaking, steel bands beating out calypso campaign songs, beach parties, television commercials, and political dealings. Only when the schools had not been able to open fully following the federal court order to admit the children of aliens had it hovered on the verge of being voiced.

The Virgin Islanders were justly proud of the high percentage of their citizenry who had participated in the election. But there were as many or more adult, tax-paying residents who did not participate, although many of them went to the rallies and picnics, because they were not eligible to vote. These people, men and women from "down island," who had been attracted from their poverty-stricken birthplaces by the boom in the American Virgins, had become so many in number that they were crucial to the islands' economic well-being. But they had no suffrage. Only quite a lot of suffering. And so far as the candidates were concerned, they might have been thought not to exist.

9. The "Down-Island Mon"

"All unfree in the Danish West Indies are from today free." That is what they say Peter von Scholten shouted down from the ramparts of Frederiksted Fort on July 2, 1848, to the massed thousands of rebellious slaves below. But neither his proclamation in the night nor King Christian VI's subsequent emancipation decree really did make the blacks "free." Of economic necessity, they remained largely bound to their former owners, and they also remained voiceless in the affairs of government—a condition that was to last, as we have seen, for eighty-eight years. By 1972, the descendants of the slaves—Americans since 1917—and the mainland Americans who had come to share the islands' sun and exploit their profits had allowed a new kind of human bondage to develop in their society. On this new slavery the prosperity of the islands rests today, just as the Danish sugar-and-cotton economy depended on chattel slavery.

We have noted that the money-spinning runaway development of the Virgins has fouled the harbors, ruined the beaches, eroded the hillsides, created slums, and generally turned the place into a textbook example of environmental despoliation. But none of this damage is so serious and seemingly intractable as the simultaneously created human cancer of a community of thousands of alien "non-persons," who have built the condominiums and hotels, raked the "sun-drenched beaches," mixed the *piña coladas,* cooked the meals, worked in the warehouses, crewed on the charter boats, trucked the tax-free goodies, and dug the ditches, until recently utterly dependent on their employers for their continued stay in the Virgins.

Back in 1940, when the Virgin Islands still were in the poorhouse stage, 8,720 residents had jobs. By 1960, even though the boom had begun, the number had increased to only 10,800. But the skyrocketing decade after 1960 made the wholesale importation of outside labor necessary. The use of imported labor on the islands was not new. In the sugar-growing days of the first half of this century, hands would come at planting time and at the harvest from the British possessions farther down the Antilles chain to make some money. But after 1960, the need was different and of indefinite duration. Workers by the thousands flocked to St. Thomas and St. Croix from St. Kitts, Anguilla, Nevis, Antigua, and other nearby islands, and even from as far away as Trinidad, off the Venezuelan coast. By early 1971, the number of people working in the Virgins was estimated at about 36,000—an increase in the work force of nearly 250 per cent in a decade. More than half of these people came from "down island." These aliens held (and still hold) more than 90 per cent of the construction jobs and 60 per cent of the jobs in the hotels, beach clubs, bars, and restaurants; they were doing virtually all of the domestic household work, and, as earlier noted, filled more than half of the openings created by the liberal subsidies granted under the Industrial Incentive Program to make jobs for Virgin Islanders. Wages paid to these people were not high—especially by stateside standards—but $1.50 to $2.50 an hour looked great to men and women used to working for $1.50 to $2.50 a day.*

* Per capita income on Antigua, highest in the Lesser Antilles outside of the Virgins, is $240 a year; on the American Virgins it is at least $3,400.

The legal non-citizen workers—known in the parlance of the Virgins as "bonded aliens" because until 1970 their employers had to pay a $10 certification fee, or "bond"—were admitted into the territory under provisions of the Immigration Act to fill jobs that, in the opinion of the U.S. Department of Labor, no U.S. citizens were "willing, qualified, and able to fill." In view of the enormous demands of the tourist trade and the fact that the government of the Virgin Islands was padding the public payrolls and absorbing the majority of the native labor force, such jobs existed by the thousands. As of late 1971, there were nearly 13,000 adult aliens certified to fill them.

There is a smaller group of workers on the islands who are known as "resident aliens," legal immigrants who were lucky enough to come to the Virgins before passage of the 1968 Immigration Act, when the immigration quotas for Britain were high and unfilled. These people, who have all the rights of citizens except the vote, can eventually become American citizens through the naturalization process—like an immigrant Greek, or Pakistani, or Guatemalan on the mainland. But not the bonded aliens. Although nearly all of them apply for "permanent status" soon after arrival, fewer than fifty a year achieve it, and these few gain admission through one of the top "preferences" the law lays down for immigrant visas (professionals, spouse of a citizen, dependents of persons with permanent status). Most of the bonded aliens on the Virgin Islands are skilled and unskilled labor, a category the Immigration people put at the bottom of the list—"sixth preference." In 1969, only twenty-four "sixth-preference" applicants *from all of the West Indies* were accepted as immigrants into the United States.

So the bonded alien has scarcely a hope of emulating the more than 45 million people who emigrated to the U.S. mainland from 1820 to the present to dig the canals, build the railroads, mine the coal, make the steel, and break the prairies. Instead, he and his fellows form a very large unassimilable lump of permanently temporary residents of U.S. territory for whom no one in the Virgin Islands or in the federal government has done much and whose presence, too much of the time, the Virgin Islanders pretend to ignore.

Yet, their presence cannot be ignored, for it is not a sometime thing. Even though the laws that allow them to work on the Virgins relate to "temporary labor," most of the aliens have been on the islands for more than five years, and some for eight to ten years; if the tourist business holds up, they will be on the islands for years to come. But still looked upon as "temporary," the aliens are denied most social services, including welfare. Theoretically, they are eligible for public housing, but there is not enough even for native Virgin Islanders. It is next to impossible for them to get bank loans. They have difficulty buying property. And when the government goes into one of its sporadic slum-clearing efforts, it is the aliens who are evicted from their shacks. Until September, 1970, they had to pay to send their children to parochial or private school. And until May, 1970, they were entirely at the mercy of the employer who had "bonded" them. If they lost their jobs for any reason, they were supposed to leave the islands within five days, although many stayed illegally. The May, 1970, change gave the bonded alien a sixty-day grace period, during which he could draw unemployment compensation, to find a job. But if he was unsuccessful he then had to leave. In the summer of 1971, the regulations were again changed, giving all aliens then under bond "indefinite" certification, certainly a more satisfactory status from their point of view but a makeshift solution that does not attack the basic problem.

Besides having none of the rights of citizens, the alien worker, legal or illegal, is an outsider in Virgin Islands society. The native islander looks down on him; he is blamed for the increase in crime; he is a hostage to bureaucratic red tape; and he lives in the most dreadful housing imaginable. Decent housing for people with low incomes, as noted earlier in this book, is one of the islands' most serious deficiencies. But the situation of the native poor seems idyllic compared to that of the aliens, almost all of whom live in hibiscus-framed squalor. Their "houses" are tarpaper shacks, packing crates, ancient wooden bungalows partitioned into tiny, separately rented rooms, old sheds and outbuildings, and, on St. Croix, the ruins of volcanic-rock slave rows on abandoned plantations. A reporter for *Look* writing about the alien problem in 1970 said that he found four people living in a derelict bus beside the road connecting Frederiksted and Christiansted—and paying rent. They were still there in late 1971.

Social, Educational Research and Development, Inc. (SERD), a Silver Spring, Maryland, survey firm, did a thorough and broad-based study of the alien situation for the Office of Economic Opportunity in 1969 that vividly underlined the deprivation of the alien workers. Sixty per cent of the aliens' dwellings examined by the SERD staff contained less than 200 square feet of floor space and 28 per cent less than 100 square feet. Most of these tiny spaces were occupied by more than one person. Eighty-seven per cent of the people questioned did not have access to hot water in their "houses," 59 per cent did not have inside toilets, 43 per cent did not have any running water, 42 per cent did not have bathtubs or showers, 37 per cent did not have refrigerators, and 21 per cent did not even have tables and chairs. The percentages tell only part of the story. "Access" to water may mean a walk of 50 to 100 yards to a communal tap. And access to a bath or shower may mean sharing the facilities with eight or ten people. All this for $40 and up a month. One woman told a questioner, "Aliens have to pay blood money for house rent. A room 10 by 10 and three people in it have to pay $20 each per week. Some on the floor, yet has to pay."

It is no wonder, then, that the lack of decent housing is the most frequent complaint of the alien worker, who usually has left better housing accomodations, if poorer job prospects, on his home island to come to the Virgins to work. But the "down-island mon" who comes to the islands is no illiterate floater attracted only by money, and he is philosophical about his sordid living conditions. "When you want to get ahead," one of them said, "the road is rough."

The SERD survey drew a skeletal portrait of a "typical" bonded alien, showing him to be typically British West Indian in background and mores:

> He is a male in his late 20's or early 30's. He is not married, but living with a woman. He has been in the Virgin Islands about five years. He is fairly well educated, at least in terms of Virgin Islands standards. [Ninety-two per cent of the aliens SERD studied had more that six years of schooling, compared to 52 per cent of adult Virgin Islanders.] He visits his home island three or four times a year and sends home about $48 a month. He works in construction at a salary of $1.50 an hour. He does not belong to a labor union. He has two children, one of whom was born in the Virgin Islands and the other "off island." His contacts with and the services he has received from public and private agencies are minimal.

Had its researchers been able to ferret out the percentages at the time the survey was made, there was one chance in three that SERD's typical alien was living illegally in the Virgin Islands. Being illegally resident was easy. For generations, West Indians have visited back and forth among the islands. Everyone has relatives spread throughout the Antilles chain. And even though visas have been required for more than a generation, almost any visitor to the Virgins could just stay on, unquestioned, when his visa expired. Or he could come in illegally in the first place by island schooner from the nearby islands—British Tortola is only three miles of open water from St. John—and land in some unpoliced cove. But most often, the illegal became "illegal" when he lost the job that had given him bonded status and melted into the alien community, where he was physically unidentifiable.

Until the late winter of 1971, the presence of illegal aliens on the islands was more or less ignored by the government but was exploited as cheap labor by a large group of unscrupulous employers. At a conference on alien problems held in Charlotte Amalie in December, 1969, Alfred Hayes, a St. Croix businessman, asked to estimate the percentage of illegal workers on employers' payrolls, said, "If there was a percentage more than 100, I would say that. I think every employer at one time or another has had one or more illegal employees. Some people are illegal all the time, not because they are willful on this, because there's no solution to it. You can't operate a business here and have non-citizens working for you and be legal all the time. It just is not possible."

The Virgin Islands government slackly left the problem of illegal immigrants to the U.S. Immigration Service; the Immigration Service had only a few enforcement agents in the islands, and they seemed to have other things to do. Now and then, when spasms of civic virtue seized them, the Virgin Islands authorities would stage "roundups," by stopping trucks carrying large crews of construction workers or descending on the slums in which the immigrants lived and demanding that everyone produce his papers. Those who did not have the "green cards" that authorized them to work were carted off to jail or sent packing to their home islands. Since the Virgin Islands police are notoriously ham-handed, these roundups were mostly brutal affairs, but the number rounded up seldom was large. A much-publicized action in June, 1969, gathered in only a few more than 100 "illegals."

The picayune results of the roundups gave credence to the general notion that there really were not all that many illegals on the islands. SERD's survey estimated their number between 2,500 and 4,000. These were conservative figures, as time would tell; yet, in 1969 some officials said they were too high to believe. But, then, the officials paid little attention to the whole alien situation, let alone the presence of illegals.

With what can only be described as heavy irony, the SERD report on the condition of the aliens observed: "Generally, the temporary alien community is not strongly identified with Virgin Islands society." The unfortunate fact is that the alien, illegal or bonded, has not been strongly identified with any society. He has attachments to the Virgins, where he hopes to be able to stay but probably won't; he has attachments as well to his home island, where he may have a wife and family in addition to the woman and family he has on St. Thomas or St. Croix. He is personally and socially disorganized.

Herein lies danger for the full fabric of island society, the tacit recognition of which may have been the key to the refusal of all of the gubernatorial candidates in the 1970 election campaign to discuss the alien problem. John McCollum, president of SERD, thinks that there are the "ingredients of an explosion" present. "The people are cut off completely from the community," he told *Look*. "This is a classic case of alienation. Remember, they don't compare themselves to how poorly they lived back on their home island but to how life is in the Virgin Islands." Most native Virgin Islanders treat the alien as a lesser human being. A common epithet for him is "garot," an imaginary predatory bird that is supposed to fly from its home island to other islands and eat everything in sight before flying home. Although he is "different" only in having been born under a different flag, the citizen callously pays the alien substandard wages, educates his children only under duress, blames him—possibly with some reason—for the increase in crime, and closes him out from most of the public services and facilities for which he helps to pay. There are no aliens on any of the dozens of boards, commissions, and other organizations that concern themselves with the affairs of the islands and their people. Their own two bodies, the Alien Interest Movement on St. Thomas and the United Alien Association on St. Croix, are largely crying-towel organizations whose leaders can carry complaints to officialdom but accomplish little because they lack political clout. The alienation of the aliens was underlined when a Non-Citizens Commission was formed in February, 1969, in accordance with a resolution of the legislature, to study their status and problems. No aliens were appointed to it.

The gross nature of the alien problem was startlingly demonstrated in the late winter and spring of 1971 when Governor Evans, shortly after taking office, got the Department of Justice to send him a special crew of Immigration agents to attack the illegal-alien situation. Apparently he and others in government had decided the situation had gotten out of hand. Teamed with the local police, the Immigration men, in the middle of the night of February 28, began a carefully planned sweep of the islands. In the first two weeks, 1,400 illegals were picked up—so many as to indicate that the police and Immigration had known who they were and where they were all the time. The procedure followed was about the same as that used in previous but much smaller operations: Everyone found without proper documentation was taken to jail and then told to get off the islands as quickly as possible. On St. Thomas, the detainees were put in the lockup of 300-year-old Fort Christian, a place so noisome that even down-and-out rumheads complain about being held there.

None of the token roundups prior to 1971 had elicited serious complaint from the alien community. But the size and vigor of Evans's swoop brought an angry reaction from bonded aliens whose friends, relatives, and fellow workmen were suddenly dragged in and sent home. Brief strikes flared up on St. Croix, including walkouts at Hess Oil and Harvey

Alumina, where there had been some illegals on the payroll. The head of the Virgin Islands Amalgamated Workers Union, Cephus Rogers, a native islander, wrote to Governor Evans and charged that many of those expelled had been assured by their employers that the necessary certification would be gotten for them. Rogers also charged that some employers were paying their workers less than the minimum wage and that those with illegal aliens on their payrolls were withholding income tax and Social Security deductions and not paying them to the government. (A U.S. Department of Labor examination of 113 establishments in 1970 found that 3,197 workers were getting less than the minimum wage of $1.30 an hour and that 3,166 were getting the minimum wage. Virtually all of the people in both groups were aliens.)

The United Alien Association and the Alien Interest Movement called on officials of other islands of the West Indies to protest the "inhumane treatment" of their citizens. Some did. Donald Halstead, Antigua's Minister of Home Affairs, pointed out to Governor Evans that the aliens contributed to the prosperity of the Virgin Islands and that precipitately returning them to their home islands would cause problems, noting that Antigua's unemployment rate was already 40 per cent. Robert Bradshaw, prime minister of St. Kitts-Nevis-Anguilla, came personally to Charlotte Amalie to try to persuade the governor to allow the illegals to remain. Evans blandly told his fellow West Indians that the roundup was a federal matter and out of his hands, although, according to the Immigration and Naturalization Service officials in Washington, the governor had asked Justice, which controls immigration, for the cleanup. Affected West Indian governments even went to the State Department, without result. "They never talked to us officially," a State Department spokesman carefully said.

This roundup did not stop after two weeks. Other thousands were found and expelled, some of them people who had been on the islands for many years. One reporter talked to a construction worker from Anguilla, waiting for transportation home, who told him that he had been employed on the Virgins for more than twelve years. By the end of June, 1971, when the roundup ceased, some eight thousand had been sent packing—nearly 10 per cent of the estimated population of the islands and 13 per cent of the number of people counted in the Census of 1970. Despite the harshness of the sweep, there was but one instance of violence. A distraught Trinidadian burst into a motel room occupied by two stateside Immigration agents one night and started shooting. He wounded one of the agents, who then managed to shoot the intruder dead. But even though there was only one overt incident, deep and widespread bitterness was left in the roundup's wake among those aliens who remained. George Goodwin, president of the Alien Interest Movement, said, "Is it any wonder that seeds of distrust and disenchantment are growing throughout the West Indies? If the Virgin Islands are, in President Kennedy's phrase, a 'showcase of democracy,' this is no way to display it."

The discovery that nearly eight thousand people had been living illegally on the Virgin Islands shocked many. However, it was only further evidence of the slipshod methods and inefficient operations of the Virgin Islands government in general and of its grasp of the alien situation in particular. And it has learned little from that experience. After the roundup had ended, Governor Evans met with Premier George Walters of Antigua and other British West Indian officials and issued a pious statement asserting that he recognized "the necessity and desirability of having a labor supply that will permit the expansion of the economy of the Virgin Islands of the United States," and that "this additional labor supply can come and would be welcomed from our neighboring islands."

During the period of the roundup the new "indefinite"

certification procedure was announced and the registration of the bonded aliens begun. An official told the *Daily News* in April that there were about 12,000 eligible for the new status. In June, however, the U.S. Department of Labor announced in Washington—perhaps there rather than Charlotte Amalie so as to minimize embarrassment to Virgin Islands bureaucrats—that 15,000 aliens had qualified for the "indefinite" category, and another 1,000 were eligible—a third more than the Virgin Islands government thought there were. This Labor Department figure was probably accurate, even though only 13,000 have so far signed up for certification.

The new employment regulations for aliens contained a provision that, combined with the expulsion of the illegals, put the employment situation in the islands in alarming perspective: The certified aliens were the only aliens (other than wives and children on the islands who could qualify) who were going to be available. In this situation, the expulsion of the illegal aliens, virtually all of whom had jobs of one kind or another, meant that the available pool of labor had been cut by more than one third. There were problems among the resort owners and others during the 1971–72 "season," even though some illegals had started sneaking back.

The reaction of the employers to the roundup of the illegals ranged from dismay to anger. In the first week after the roundup began, construction on a badly needed junior-senior high school to serve the rapidly growing eastern end of St. Thomas stopped when the work force was reduced from 37 men to three. A St. Croix construction company lost 98 workers out of 130. Hotels, bars, and restaurants were especially hard hit. At the Virgin Isle Hilton on St. Thomas, dining room waiters were assigned forty "covers" each instead of the usual twenty-five. Robert Bridgman, president of the St. Thomas Hotel Association, told the *Daily News,* "They tell us to recruit locally, in Puerto Rico, and on the mainland. That has been tried, and so far it has not been successful. The Virgin Islander has never gravitated toward the service trades of this sort and certainly is not breaking down our doors now. Puerto Ricans have often been excellent, but they usually don't feel happy and eventually drift away. And too many mainlanders come down for a few months and, after enjoying a paid vacation, pack up again—often before they are fully enough trained to be worth what you've been paying them."

Is there a solution to this dilemma? If so, it is not readily apparent. The suggestion that aliens be given representation in the legislature but with no vote was rejected at a conference of the Non-Citizens Commission. Congress could amend the Immigration Law to make it possible for some or all of the aliens now on the islands to become legal immigrants, but Congress moves warily with immigration legislation and, anyway, it has so far shown little concern for this group of black foreigners out in the Caribbean. Even if such a law were passed, it would have to be hedged about with restrictions to keep the new immigrants on the islands—for many, if not most, probably would take off for the mainland as soon as they obtained permanent status. And giving the aliens full rights of citizens would be political dynamite, since the number of aliens of voting age is close to, if not more than, the number of enfranchised native blacks.

So, the Virgin Islands alien population remains a problem unique in contemporary American society, a sad problem and a shameful one. These bonded people are a little better off today than they were before the changes of 1971, but essentially their lives under what can be justly described as economic and political enslavement are as they were poignantly described to the 1969 conference of the Non-Citizens Commission by Tom Browne, president of the United Alien Association:

We wonder what will be our destiny, always apprehensive that any day the bond will be terminated, for it is true to say, "For a little while he was here and in a moment he is no more." The insecurity of our existence alarms us, because even though we exist for as much as twenty years in this bonded condition we know not what tomorrow may bring. Of course we would like to share in the economy in other ways, by owning our own homes, stocks, bonds, and shares in the corporations that we have helped to prosper, but how? These things we are unable to accomplish if we are bonded. We would like to live here, reside here completely and call the place we have helped to develop our home, but how can we if we are bonded? We would like to be able to help in the enforcement of the laws so that the Virgin Islands would be the best place in the world to live, but how can we if we are bonded?

10. *Relax and Enjoy It?*

One of the things that seemed to be bothering people I talked to, when I went back for a second look at the Virgins in the autumn of 1971, was what had happened to a story about the islands that *Life* magazine was known to have had in the works. In the spring of that year, a *Life* photographer and a reporter had spent nearly two months on St. Thomas and St. Croix. Both men got what they were looking for: The photographer, scenes of tropical beauty—and tropical despoliation; the reporter, facts that showed deep flaws in "Our Caribbean Gems."

The *Life* writer, Greg Walter, a hard-driving journalist, some months later told me about the story's development and fate. Among the stateside people he talked to after his return from the Virgins was Stewart Udall. There were two meetings, both in Udall's Overview Group offices, half a block from the White House. Walter said, "I was very soft the first time, because what I really wanted was a talk with Henry Kimelman, and Kimelman wasn't available for the first meeting. [Kimelman, beach-miner Sidney Kessler's son-in-law, had been Udall's special assistant at Interior and is now head of a large development firm in the Virgins as well as Udall's associate at Overview.] A week later I went to 1700 Pennsylvania Avenue for the second interview. Kimelman didn't show this time, either. So I decided to put the hard questions to Udall himself. I asked him about the $550,000 Halprin contract that he had approved when he was Secretary of the Interior, and about his connection with Halprin in Overview, and about Kimelman's connection with it. He got furious. At one point he yelled at me, 'You're not going to use Stew Udall to sell *Life* magazine.' Then he cooled down and started talking about people he knew on *Life,* like the publisher and one of the senior editors. He never really said it, but I got the implication that he would speak to them about the story. I went back to New York and wrote it."

Producing an article for *Life* is a tortuous process. Walter did an original draft, then did a second, shorter version to go with the working layout of pictures, and then did a third to fit the exact limits of a rectangular "box" to be used with a four-page color spread of pictures. Walter said that the type for the story was set, the picture layouts completed, all of the technical processes finished, and the feature, with Walter's unflattering 7,000-word story about the Virgins, ready for the presses.

"At *Life,*" Walter told me, "you have a *guru,* a friend on the editorial side who will bird-dog your stuff through the editorial and production processes and push it until it gets into the magazine. Otherwise, it will never get in. Honest. Mine had told me that this story was all ready—and, in fact, I saw the finished layouts—but after a while he called me and said things didn't look too hopeful, and then a couple of weeks later he called me and said that the piece and the pictures were never going to run. Nobody ever gave me any reason, and believe me, I asked. My *guru* didn't know—and couldn't find out. The next week I quit."

Walter, who when I talked to him was an investigative reporter for the Philadelphia *Evening Bulletin,* offers no opinion about who was responsible for *Life*'s not using the story on which tens of thousands of dollars had been spent. He is

sure that there was, in his words, "political pressure," involved in killing the article that *Life* had planned to run
under the heading "The Rape of the U.S. Virgins."

(Although an acquaintance of mine in *Life*'s Washington
bureau knew that I was writing a book about the Virgins,
any resemblance to its title, which was specified in my contract with Praeger Publishers in March, 1971, about the time
Walter was gathering facts for his aborted piece, is, I am
persuaded, not only coincidental but confirmingly inevitable.
Walter—or the *Life* editor who wrote the headline—and I
both knew a criminal act when we saw one.)

* * *

"We too are 'natural objects.' "

The words of former Senator Julius Sprauve, describing
himself and his fellow St. Johnians, echo. The aging man
who wrote them in sorrow and anger at his discovery of a
Rockefeller's "different morality" had earned the right to
respect for his views on those mornings when he rowed himself the four miles across Pillsbury Sound to St. Thomas to
fulfill his duties in the Virgin Islands legislative sessions he
never missed. (More honor to him if it was true, as a friend
of his told me, that he took to the oars on mornings after a
late night's conviviality made him miss the ferry.) But the
poignancy of the words extends beyond the plight of St. John
landowners confronted by an attempted land grab in the
name of conservation. There the issue was immediate and
simple. Others are not so clear-cut, and the over-all situation
is devilish in its complexity. The criminal act committed in
these islands has claimed many victims and involved many
perpetrators and accessories after the fact. In fact, both island
society and the larger political society of the United States
have suffered and are to blame.

The natural objects that comprise the Virgin Islands include the rocks, the coral reefs and their flashing, sunlit fish,

the sand, the mangrove swamps, the hillsides, the trees and sweet-scented tropical flora, the native black haves and the native black have-nots, the so-called royal families, white and colored, the continentals, including the ones who had it when they came and the ones who came to make it, the aliens, and the sea around all of them. The rape of the American Virgins has had adverse effects on all these natural objects, from the sea itself to the individuals and families and even the business enterprises that appeared to profit most in the runaway growth. Here there is no battle in which those who would save the landscape and the view are poised in Sierra Club combat against those who would cut down the trees or build roads through them for the sake of the people or the gain. Here, in the real laboratory of these three small American islands, can be seen plain, whole, and frightening the effects on all living things of reckless development. It takes no great leap of the imagination to transfer the course of events to other spoiling or still unspoiled areas of the world. Difficult as they may be to sift from the complexity of cause and the equal complexity of effect, there are lessons here.

The varying kinds of environmental despoliation or attempts at ecological protectionism on the three islands have been described in earlier chapters. The special degradation of the alien workers has had a chapter to itself. Now it is time to consider the over-all cost to all of the people of this symbolically significant, far out of proportion to its size, U.S. territory.

The tax, to use the word in its original sense, has been levied most heavily on the native population. They have suffered new kinds of discrimination and disorienting cultural change. In two articles in the *Daily News* in September, 1971, Dr. Lesmore Emanuel, a native-born sociologist at the College of the Virgin Islands, deplored the damage done to traditional customs that once enriched the lives of all island residents and charmed visitors. He wrote:

Our traditional courtesy is giving way to brusque, crude, even vulgar habits of speech. Our concern for human beings is giving way to an outlook that places undue emphasis on material things. The large house, the fine car, the costly furniture are becoming more and more important to us while aged parents and helpless relatives are neglected. We are caught up in the scramble for prestige, the material goods of the West, only to find, when we do achieve them, that a certain vital element is missing. . . . We experience a certain emptiness, a sense of loss that mocks us.

Dr. Emanuel went on to say that "to alleviate the situation" natives resort to "alcohol, marijuana, the movies and television" to shut out temporarily "the aspects of a society and a way of life that have become unbearable," and added:

Why must we run away? The answer is plain enough. We have abandoned our way of life and have adopted an inferior substitute. The sad fact is that many of us never realized that we had a valid culture, a satisfying way of life, and took unto ourselves the entire way of life of Western man. We did not even stop to question whether or not it was altogether good for us. We are finding out now when it is almost too late that we have discarded a great deal of our culture and have lost heavily in the process of cultural change.

The well-to-do continentals who moved to the Virgins before the boom began or in its early years and built expensively simple houses high above the sea also have lost the "satisfying way of life" that attracted them to the islands. Day after day, the noises of construction on the hillsides below them mock the solitude they sought. (During the three months I lived in a St. Thomas hilltop house during the 1970 political campaign, the building of three houses was started on the forty-five-degree slope below.) Trucks and automobiles and mufflerless motorcycles roar by in the day and in the night. People who once never thought to lock their houses or gates now have alarm systems and guard dogs that prowl their yards and gardens for protection against robbery and assault. (On St. Croix there is a guard-dog rental agency.) These continentals once moved easily among the natives of all stations but now keep more and more to themselves, unhappy with the new unease between the races. Because of the crowds of tourists, they venture into town only when they have to.

The moneymakers have not yet been hurt, but they worry constantly about the continuation of the boom, watching tourist statistics as the natives used to watch the barometer during the hurricane season in the days before radio weather reports. Apparently there are few among them who, like Isidor Paiewonsky, worry about the mess that shop owners, builders, real estate men, hotel operators, contractors, and the rest have made of their golden islands in their unheeding pursuit of the buck. Their apparent blindness to what is happening is hard to believe; their apparent failure to link their outrageous commitment to high profits with environmental damage and the approaching obliteration of the easy grace of the Virgins is hard to accept. Perhaps deep in their hearts they are all too aware that the day may come—perhaps sooner than they think—when the tourists, not liking what they see and what they are charged, will turn elsewhere for fun in the sun. They must know that not even cruise-ship passengers, who among visitors experience the least effects, are likely to put up indefinitely with profiteering and unnecessary inconvenience. The outsider's view of First Pennsylvania Bank's economist Lawrence Murdoch in 1970 was that "Up to now the problems with electricity, water, roads, and other services have been accepted good-naturedly by most visitors as part of the islands' unspoiled charm. But as the crowding increases and tourists must pay higher and higher prices, they are likely to become less tolerant."

The racial distrust and tensions that have arisen in recent years stem directly from the despoiling growth and its social and economic ramifications. Although peculiarly Virgin Islands in origin, tone, and content, with none of the militant anger, hatred, and violence evident in many places on the mainland, this new feeling is nonetheless a serious matter, and the continuing polarization of the races and the withdrawal of many whites from day-to-day social contact with the natives can only make it worse. Interestingly, efforts by mainland blacks to carry activist messages to the Virgin Islands have had little effect. Not even Roy Innis, a native who returned to the islands in 1969 as national director of the Congress of Racial Equality and started a CORE branch on the islands, attracted many supporters. Nor have the Black Cultural Organization at the College of the Virgin Islands and the United Caribbean Association of Black People on St. Croix made much headway in building a militant movement. These groups are largely frustrated and preoccupied with divided strategies. But that is the situation now. What may happen in time to come? Henry Howard, a former British Colonial Office administrator in the West Indies, now living on St. Thomas, wrote in the American *Foreign Service Journal* of January, 1972, that talk of black power "has alarmed many of the wealthy White Americans. It has alarmed the Merchant Princes of St. Thomas and St. Croix, both black and white, who see in white tourism the only economic future for the islands."

He went on to say:

If there has as yet been no successful projection of [militant black] philosophy, it lies uncomfortably on the stomachs of many Virgin Islanders, both black and white. These prefer not to talk about it. They applaud articles in the American press extolling the virtues of the islands as a tourist haven. They deprecate the articles that paint a gloomy picture of the racial and economic position. They draw comfort from the blue license plates which proclaim "American Paradise." They are muddled about Black Power and vaguely apprehensive.

"Vaguely apprehensive" well describes the general condition of many residents, white and black, as they look around them and see not only evidence of a new edginess affecting relations between the races but also all the ugly things that have happened to the islands. Why did these things happen? many of the more thoughtful are beginning to ask. How did they happen so fast? Who is to blame?

* * *

Congressmen and senators whose constituents have mining, oil, fishing, grazing, timber, and similar interests fight for places on the committees on Interior and Insular Affairs. Early in this century, getting on the territorial subcommittees was also worth a fight for these groups controlled Oklahoma, New Mexico, Arizona, Alaska, Hawaii, the Philippines, Puerto Rico, Guam, Samoa, and, after 1917, the three little Virgins—altogether a pretty big and rich parish. Even in the 1950s, a subcommittee assignment was important, as Puerto Rico did not achieve commonwealth status until 1952 and Alaska and Hawaii did not become states until 1959. That not much attention was paid by these subcommittees to the three tiny islands in the Caribbean inhabited largely by black people—and not many of them—is perhaps understandable. Members had bigger fish to fry.

Curiously, though, one of the big fish fryers, Wayne N. Aspinall, of Palisade, Colorado, now chairman of the House Committee on Interior and Insular Affairs, did pay attention. Before he moved up to the committee chairmanship in January, 1959, he had been chairman of the subcommittee on territories and insular affairs and had visited the Virgins frequently. Even after his elevation to head of the parent group, he kept a close eye and a controlling tether on what the Congress did about the territory. In effect, the Virgins became something of an Aspinall private preserve—unfortunately for their rational development, since conservation and environmental protection are not his forte. Paul Brooks, a leading conservationist, wrote an angry article for the March, 1963, issue of *Harper's* about Aspinall's holding up passage of the Wilderness Act. The magazine headed the piece "How one powerful man . . . can defy the will of Congress and jeopardize a natural asset of incalculable worth." Aspinall's attitude toward the Virgins was less adamantine. In fact, he looked benignly on as the runaway boom of the 1960s took place, just as he has looked on destructive lumbering, strip mining, industrial grazing of meat animals on public lands, and commercial development of unspoiled areas in the continental United States.

Where were all the other members of Congress? I asked Representative Phillip Burton of San Francisco, who became chairman of the subcommittee in 1971. Our conversation took place during the early months of 1972, when Congress had before it legislation to end the strike of the West Coast longshoremen and there were problems among the California *chicanos,* with whose affairs Burton has been involved since he was a member of the California legislature. Between telephone calls, the chairman said, "I guess it's true we haven't paid enough attention to the Virgins. We've had in the past a couple of chairmen of the subcommittee who were nice guys, but they never got into the islands' problems. They just left them to Wayne."

Burton by the spring of 1972 had been in the Virgins only twice, and, although he has put pressure on government officials there and has asked hard questions of some of the subsidized industries, his heart is still in San Francisco. There is talk on Capitol Hill that the subcommittee may be abolished because of the meager responsibilities left to it. (The importance of congressional committees and subcommittees can be judged by the size of the staffs attached to them. There is only one staff assistant in the House concerned with the Virgins, and in the Senate one man keeps an eye on them in addition to other and wider duties.) The record of the executive department is no better than that of the Congress. The Navy's single-minded rule was colonial and unresponsive to local needs. The first civilian governor, Paul Pearson, tried and made a decent beginning. But the quality of the presidential appointees who filled the twenty-seven-year gap between "the experimental Quaker" and rum-merchant Ralph Paiewonsky ranged from good to bad to horrid. Under Republicans and Democrats alike, the Virgin Islands were treated as a nice place to send somebody who wasn't important enough to be an ambassador.

Whoever was appointed governor, the executive responsibility for the affairs of the Virgin Islands rested in Washington with one or another cabinet department. First it was the Navy, then, in the early civilian years, the Department of the Interior, the Department of War, and the Navy all had involvements there. Now, Interior, except for controlling the submerged lands around the islands and the National Parks on St. John and Buck Island off St. Croix, and maintaining a resident government comptroller, is more a service agency for the Virgins than anything else. Even its Office of Territories, which formerly kept an eye on the remaining U.S. territories (in addition to the Virgins: Guam, Samoa, and the Trust Territory of the Pacific, generally known as Micronesia), has been abolished and its responsibilities turned over to a deputy assistant secretary, lately loaned to Interior by the Department of State. There is one member of his staff who works with Virgin Islands affairs—and his role is that of liaison man for the islands.

The post–World War II neglect of the Virgin Islands has come full circle. Once ignored by Congress and the executive

branch because nobody cared, they are now virtually over-
looked because everybody is too busy. And just when someone should be looking closely.

The only watcher out of Washington is Comptroller Ross,
whom the islanders would like to get rid of. A draft constitution they adopted in 1964 called for the comptroller to be a
Virgin Islands official appointed by the governor. Another
draft constitution drawn up early in 1972 includes a similar
provision. Only a few provisions of the 1964 draft, including
the popular election of the islands' governor, were passed
into law by Congress. Congressional sentiment would indicate that a similar piecemeal approach will be taken to the
1972 draft.

There have been spot examinations of limited nature done
by the General Accounting Office (GAO), Congress's fiscal
monitoring service. In 1970, prompted by Comptroller Ross's
report for 1969, the GAO examined the financial operations
of the islands and found, as Ross had, that the Virgin Islands
government did not know how much money it had in the
bank, how many checks were outstanding, how much was
owed to it, or how much it had invested in land, buildings,
and equipment, and also that it had no reliable records of
materials and supplies on hand.

The GAO report, published in March, 1971, was entitled
"Financial Management of Virgin Islands Needs Substantial
Improvement," an understatement that was kind compared
to a stinging letter Ross sent to Governor Evans on March
31, 1971, in which he cited twelve egregious "errors" he and
his staff had caught in their examination of 1970 operations.
The list was as follows:

1. Taxes held in escrow were understated by $8,910,216.
2. Reserves for estimated total disability payments were understated by $108,773.
3. Interest revenue on time deposits was understated by
   $1,756,970.

4. Accrued interest receivable was understated by $485,033.
5. Amount due to other funds was overstated by $222,088.
6. Receipts totaling $876,920 were apparently erroneously reported as "Miscellaneous Revenues."
7. Accounts receivable for U.S. Customs dues were understated by $1,942,261.
8. Interest earned on Conservation Fund No. 485 was duplicated in the amount of $204,356.
9. Interest earned on Unemployment Fund No. 643 time deposits was duplicated in the amount of $267,139.
10. Although capital expenditures were reported as $10,797,706, the fixed-assets accounts increased only $2,895,621.
11. Purchase of $1,000,000 of Tennessee Valley Authority bonds was included twice in Investments.
12. As of June 30, 1970, there were 252 accounts overexpended and/or overencumbered totaling $6,508,050.95. A further review made as of December 31, 1970, disclosed 374 accounts overdrawn totaling $4,446,902.92.

The Comptroller went on to say to the Governor:

Any system that would permit errors of this magnitude to go undetected is grossly inadequate. You are already aware that bank accounts have not been properly reconciled for years, that control over receivables is very poor, and that the procedures for payment of bills are cumbersome, inefficient, and are hurting the credit of the Government. . . . In my opinion your present term of office will expire before reasonable compliance [with federal law regulating territorial fiscal management] can be reached unless some drastic action is taken.

Whatever the failings of presidents and their appointed governors, the Congress of the United States, and the Department of the Interior, the greater part of the blame for the fiscal mess just described and the general mess the islands are in must be placed on the citizen-residents themselves. Of this blame, the larger portion falls on the black natives, who have for so long allowed their affairs to be run so highhandedly. Not that the continentals are blameless. These people, who make up the islands' smallest minority, have great influence on what goes on. Their influence is exercised behind the scenes, however, since most continentals keep aloof from the rough-and-tumble of politics, while criticizing the natives among themselves for their ineffectual conduct. One white resident, who came to the Virgins just after World War II, told me'that "there is a grand ineptness in the Virgin Islander's way of doing things."

There is some truth in this observation—and there are reasons for it that have to be thought about.

At a conference on "The Evolving Status of the Virgin Islands," in 1968, Roy C. Macridis, of Brandeis University, summing up one panel discussion, said, "The conference seemed to agree—and overwhelmingly—that both the substance and the forms of what are called 'administrative tutelage'—another name for colonialism—should be eliminated. Within the Constitution, self-government ought to become a reality. The Virgin Islands should be placed on a par with the states."

When Professor Macridis used the word "colonialism," he was talking straight to an important point, for the Virgin Islanders have been under some kind of colonial restraint throughout their history. Their experience of nearly three hundred years of colonialism could have a great deal to do with the problems they now find themselves facing.

A high-ranking official of the government of India once told an American ambassador to that country, "You don't know what it is like to live under colonialism. It does something to your soul." It also does something to the self-reliance and the self-restraint needed for independent government, as has been demonstrated throughout the world since just after World War II, when the colonial powers pulled out of so many of their overseas possessions. Almost everywhere, they left their former charges to their own devices, inadequately equipped for freedom. The troubles of Africa, the

Middle East, India and Pakistan, and the new republics of the West Indies can be laid in large part at the doorstep of former colonial masters who did not take measures to build in the peoples they ruled the qualities of character and the experience necessary for eventual roles in free states. It was as if the mother bird did not teach her fledglings to fly.

The analogy applies to the U.S. Territory of the Virgin Islands. For years the islanders were treated much more cavalierly by American officials acting as colonial masters than Punjabi peasants were being treated at the same time by British members of the Indian Civil Service. They were ordered about, given very few positions of trust, and generally not expected to perform well—even indulged in poor performance. Worse, the Virgin Islands natives were conned from the very beginning of American rule and, again in the world pattern, were freed from the vestiges of colonialism, when that finally took place in 1961, in what can now be seen as much too abrupt a manner for anybody's good. The American government's sudden shedding of its responsibility in the Virgins became it no more than its assumption of colonial rule.

On April 1, 1917, *Lightbourn's Mail Notes,* a Charlotte Amalie newspaper of the day, hailed the transfer of the islands from Denmark to the United States in a challenging editorial that said, "We are taken under the Stars and Stripes not as a conquered people, neither do we expect to be treated as such. . . . From this moment on, it is our flag and in every respect we demand every privilege and all the protection it stands for." Unhappily, things did not turn out that way. The treaty said that Danish citizens could opt for American citizenship after a year—but the natives were not considered Danish citizens. The treaty said that their "civil rights and political status . . . shall be determined by Congress." But what Congress first "determined," on March 3, 1917 in an Act setting up a temporary government for the

territory about to be annexed by the navy, was that the
Danish laws regulating the islands proclaimed by Frederick
VIII in 1906 and other relevant Danish laws, some dating
back hundreds of years, were to remain in effect. Then
Congress promptly forgot about its new charges, and "temporary" took on a long meaning. The natives became "non-
persons," as the aliens are today. In the early years of the
territory's existence, responsibility for the essentially colonial rule of the American Virgins was partly the business of
the president, represented by the navy governor, and partly
the responsibility of Congress, not only as lawmaker, but,
through its House and Senate committees on Interior and
Insular Affairs and their subcommittees on territorial and
insular affairs, as overseer. Eleven years of agitation against
the naval administration and persistent prodding of Congress were necessary just to get American citizenship for Virgin Islanders. It took twenty years to get universal suffrage
and the right to elect their own representatives to the municipal councils of St. Thomas-St. John and St. Croix. (The
British, whose colonial policies Americans have inveighed
against since the Stamp Act, established municipal elections
in India as early as 1882 and general elections by the Government of India Act of 1919.)

Cyril King, the unsuccessful ICM candidate for governor,
in a speech to the Christiansted Rotary Club just before the
1970 political campaign began, put his finger on an underlying cause of the natives' neglect of their own affairs. After
discussing the "scars" left by the islands' colonial past, he said
that there were still others created by "the plantation existence we once depended upon" that developed a "plantation
psychology" in too many people. "By 'plantation psychology,' " he said, "I mean calculated paternalism that stunts
the development of self-reliance, that imposes discipline but
does not develop it, that has as its base the single-track self-

interest of the plantation owner, supervisor, and manager —today they are the political bosses—and not the individual Virgin Islander."

The 1970 general election may have marked the beginning of a break away from the plantation psychology, for the voters came very close to putting a reform administration into office and gave clear indication of their attitude toward ·the entrenched Democratic bosses by not giving the machine's gubernatorial candidate enough votes even to get into the runoff. The voter reaction was an encouraging sign that the Virgin Islands' natives themselves have recognized what has been done and is being done to them and their homeland. It also may have signified that they were tired enough of legislative hanky-panky to try to end it and savvy enough to know how, for to mount a relatively effective reform movement in the brief span of ten years is an achievement that would do credit to any sophisticated mainland political constituency. Since the power their representatives won was less than absolute by quite a bit, however, the unanswered question is: Would the reformers have been able to reform, or would the temptation of office have corrupted them also?

Since 11:45 A.M., January 4, 1971, the people of the Virgin Islands have been masters of their own affairs. It was then that Dr. Melvin H. Evans raised his hand under the octagonal roof of Charlotte Amalie's old Emancipation Garden bandstand, less than a hundred feet from a large bust of King Frederick VI, in whose reign slavery on the islands ended, and was sworn in as the islands' first elective governor by Associate Justice of the Supreme Court of the United States Thurgood Marshall, the first black to serve on the nation's highest court. Secretary of Transportation John A. Volpe, representing President Nixon, and Secretary of the Interior Rogers C. B. Morton were on the platform, but their presence was symbolic only. Washington's executive hold on the Virgin Islands ended when Dr. Evans said, "So help me, God."

A discouraging aftermath of the election that brought him to Government House and broke the Democrats' control of government was that the re-elected machine senators, with the support of two new Democrats and the three Republican members, went straight back to their old ways, and the public trough, as soon as the legislature convened. One of the first bills introduced in the 1971 session would have given the legislators a whopping pay increase. Members already were receiving $9,000 a year, more than legislators' pay in thirty-eight of the fifty states—and they got this amount for seventy-five days of regular sessions and brief special sessions. The new bill called for salaries of $15,000 a year, a scale that would have put the Virgin Islands in a three-way tie with Pennsylvania and Michigan for second place on the legislative salary ladder. As an inducement to gubernatorial approval, the bill also upped Governor Evan's salary from $35,000 to $45,000, a figure surpassed only by the salaries paid to the governors of Texas, New York, and California. Although Evans, under considerable local pressure and loud protests, vetoed the measure, and there were enough ICM senators in opposition to prevent passage over his veto, the governor's disapproval was less than a ringing denunciation of treasury raiding: "The present timing of this measure—when the fiscal condition of the government is not healthy—is not in the best interests of the people of the Virgin Islands."

The legislators have had to continue to get along on their $9,000 a year—plus what other money they make from dealing in one way or another with the government—practicing law in its courts, renting property to it or leasing choice tracts from it, selling it supplies, getting tax breaks or contracts for clients, and, most important, making sure no laws are passed that might interfere with their prosperity and that of their friends. (Governor Evans, to his credit, tried to get a "conflict of interest" law passed in 1970 that, like similar stateside laws, would prevent members of the legislature and government officials from dealing with government matters that might be profitable to them. But the legislature, then still under Ottley's control, countered with a bill of its own that was as toothless as an ancient lion. Evans vetoed it, and the islands still have no law that says it is illegal to be on the government payroll and make money from it on the side.)

Besides trying to raise their own salaries and wooing the governor with the prospect of a whopping raise of his own, the legislature, ignoring the fact that government income had begun to level off, adopted a budget for 1971–72 that called for an expenditure of about $12 million more than the year's anticipated revenue—including a tax of $10.50 on every gallon of Virgin Islands rum sold on the mainland and grants expected from various federal programs. The "first elected governor" has been nearly as irresponsible. In the time he has been in office, the already unconscionably inflated government payroll has increased by about 15 per cent. There are now twenty-two lawyers, about one-quarter of all lawyers on the islands, working in the attorney general's department. And practicing law on the side.

* * *

If the islanders are to have any hope of reversing the ruinous trend of affairs and rehabilitating their relatively few acres of earthly paradise, there are a number of things that have to be done—some of them immediately.

First of all, they have to slow down and catch up; to take a hard look at the physical state they are in and figure out what to do about it. Although the Evans' administration has made a start toward building sewage-disposal systems, rebuilding and resurfacing roads, and providing more housing, schoolrooms, and hospital facilities, these programs are partially cosmetic—and not surprisingly so, since the years of neglect have made the total physical task an enormous and an enormously expensive one. True rehabilitation will take great effort and cost a great deal. Some kind of agenda has to be set and a long-range development plan devised, based on agreed-upon priorities. Whatever the pressure from the exploiters, this plan must be made to stick if the process of despoliation is to be reversed.

Probably the first item on the agenda should be straightening out the islands' fiscal affairs. At present, the territory is not getting much for its money but an overblown bureaucracy. The tax structure needs thorough overhauling—in particular the real-property tax, which brings in a piddling $2.6 million a year, a mere 3.3 per cent of all locally raised revenue. In contrast, U.S. rum drinkers contribute nearly $15 million annually through the "matching fund," while *their* real-property taxes average one third of all state and local revenues collected. Also in need of very close examination is the contribution made to government revenue by the million-odd tourists, particularly that quarter-million who come off cruise ships, crowd the streets for a few hours of "duty-free" shopping, and go on to the next glamorous stop on their itinerary. They pay no direct taxes of any kind on their purchases or activities, and how much of the $100 million they spend annually finds its way into the government treasury through local income tax collections, gross-receipts taxes on businesses, and other levies is impossible to estimate.

The desire on the part of many islanders to be placed "on a par with the states," in the words of Professor Macridis, is absolutely dependent on a realistic and thorough reform of present fiscal operations. Whether or not the islands could survive without the special privileged status they now enjoy is the first question. Whether they can expect to enjoy this status indefinitely, if they continue to abuse it, is the next. Whether, if financial privileges are to be foregone in favor of some kind of autonomous status (few want statehood and independence is unthought of), a viable non-privileged economic base can be worked out is still another. But whatever the answers in such an exercise in self-examination, it is clear that careless waste of funds must be halted at once.

It also is inescapably clear that the whole tourist business, the bone and muscle of the islands' economy, needs thorough study. It is a business over whose vagaries the islands have no control. In 1972, the Caribbean is a highly popular place to get away to, and the Virgin Islands is the most popular. On one nightmarish day early in 1972 eight ships, including the giant *Queen Elizabeth II,* put into harbor. But as the 1970s pass, might not the current popularity shift elsewhere, just as it shifted to the Virgin Islands in the 1960s? Tourism in the islands could die of its own weight. Governor Evans has said several times that sooner or later restrictions must be put on tourist traffic, but up to now nothing has been done. "There is a nagging fear on the part of many," he told a reporter for the Baltimore *Sun,* "that if you ever lose your momentum, you lose your competitive advantage." Regulation would not be easy to achieve. To place limits on the number of cruise ships docking on a given day would necessitate some kind of cooperative scheduling system with cruise ports throughout the Caribbean area and with the steamship lines themselves, and would cause all kinds of admiralty-law problems. Control of the snowballing numbers arriving by jet aircraft could be achieved if the islanders are gutsy enough not to build that jetport at Mangrove Lagoon on St. Thomas and not to enlarge Alexander Hamilton Airport on St. Croix to accommodate superjets like the Boeing 747. It might be well to adopt a philosophy that says: "Let those who want to come to visit us come by existing means and find islands they can still enjoy."

But what is a satisfactory adjunct to controlled tourism? What can take up the slack? This question is another the islanders themselves are going to have to try to answer. Subsidized industry, large and small, as noted, has not worked. Only 16 per cent of the about five thousand created jobs have been filled by natives; more than half of the rest have been filled by "down-island" aliens, creating problems for themselves and the Virgin Islands government. If the government would cut its payroll to rational size, perhaps the natives, out of necessity, would move to jobs in the new industries. But before that can happen, they need training. The public schools of the Virgin Islands and the College need to be adapted to meet existing and future needs instead of concentrating on what used to be called "academic" subjects and the liberal arts. Education has to be geared to produce technicians, artisans, and paraprofessionals instead of emulating, as it does, the educational system Thomas Babington Macaulay developed in India for the British Raj. The recent introduction of a business-administration course at the College of the Virgin Islands and the expansion of the college's nurses' training and education courses are encouraging beginnings.

In short, the Virgin Islands' future is up to the Virgin Islanders. They may complain about the government comptroller's looking over their shoulders, about remaining restrictions on spending money from the matching fund, about the fact that they cannot vote for the president and have no voting representation in Congress. But they are, nonetheless, largely free of stateside interference in their affairs. They have more freedom of action than mainland political units many times their size—and more financial resources. Their problems are large but identifiable and should not be unsolvable if the islanders—black and white, old family and newcomers—set out to solve them. The rape of the American Virgins cannot be undone but its effects can be minimized and steps can be taken to prevent a repetition of the crime, provided that there is an inclination to do more than relax and enjoy it. Instead of running advertisements in the media exhorting everybody to be friendly to the tourists, the government should be mobilizing the residents to salvage the beauty and charm of their islands by taking concerted action on all fronts. A small but not insignificant start, for example, could be made just by tidying up the place.

* * *

A year ago a program was begun among the children in the public schools that is proving change is not impossible. To see it in action, the visitor must go to the semi-arid southeastern corner of St. John, where a National Park Service nature trail runs along the shore of Salt Pond Bay, cuts across a narrow neck of land past the salt pond from which the bay got its name, and ends at the bleak, rocky beach of Drunk Bay, swept by tradewinds blowing thirty miles an hour most of the year. Along the trail are tall pipe-organ cacti, known locally as dildo cacti, and a bulbous variety known as pope's head, the fuzzy-leafed maran plant that St. Johnians once used like steel wool for scrubbing, wild nutmeg, sea grape, and mangrove trees. The open ground is covered with seaside lavender and bay pea vines that save the sandy soil from wind erosion. Laughing gulls and brown boobies float on the calm surface of the bay, and sandpipers wade in the shallows feeding on insects, worms, and small crustaceans. The landlocked salt pond itself, a broad stretch of water reddish with algae, has white foam along its shore that looks like detergent suds on a mainland stream, but the foam is salt in the process of formation. Natives used to harvest the salt in the spring after months of evaporation under the steady tradewinds had produced it.

Until recently, this trail along Salt Bay and extending to Drunk Bay (the name of which has nothing to do with intoxication but probably comes from the Dutch Creole word meaning "drowned") was seldom used. But it sees a lot of foot traffic these days, having been adopted as an open-air classroom for an imaginative and apparently extremely effective experiment in environmental studies for the schoolchildren of St. Thomas and St. John. The program is the creation of an intense continental woman, Doris Jadan, who has lived on St. John with her husband since the early 1950s and for several years has been a teacher in the island's school system. Profoundly distressed by the environmental deterioration of the islands and by the schoolchildren's near divorcement from their natural world, Mrs. Jadan in 1970 persuaded the school system to give her a year off to prepare a course that would teach Virgin Islands children about the wonders of their place under the sun. With the assistance of a federal grant, the program was begun in the 1971–72 school year for children in the fourth, fifth, and sixth grades on St. Thomas and St. John. Mrs. Jadan herself wrote most of the basic text, *Guide to the Natural History of St. John,* published by the Virgin Islands Conservation Society. With the assistance of the Department of Conservation, she also put together sets of color slides for classroom use, organized training sessions for teachers whose classes would participate in the program, and with some other teachers began a series of articles in the *Daily News* called "The Adventures of Ivan Environman," about a fictional eleven-year-old St. Johnian and the natural world around him.

Mrs. Jadan's program goes far beyond nature studies. As she told me, sitting on the patio of her beautifully simple house above Cruz Bay (after showing me baby hummingbirds in a nest behind her kitchen), "What the course is intended to do is create a recognition of the unlikely relationships of birds, fish, and man with thorns, spines, and other unpleasant things, and with wind, sand, and salt. The children can see how the spines of the dildo cactus help it adapt to its arid environs. They can be careful to step around the long black spines of a sea egg. Children can learn that man is not obliged to conquer nature, but to respect it, even when it is uncomfortable, inconvenient, or in the way."

One of the instruction sheets she prepared for the teachers expands on this theme, emphasizing the "environmental strands" of interaction and interdependence, change and continuity, adaptation and evolution. "These strands are constants that run through the Web of Life," she wrote, "and give it the satisfying order we often call the 'balance of nature'—a balance that children can appreciate as their own environmental awareness, joy, and concern help them shape an environmental ethic that will fit them into a fit environment. Effective use of the strands means use of all of the observer's senses: he smells the bay leaf at Reef Bay; he tastes the salt or salt foam from Salt Pond Bay; he feels the textures of leaves and rock and bark; he hears the difference between a mockingbird and a thrushee; he sees the gold in the golden orb spider's web. These things one does not forget."

Although the youngsters from St. John itself are learning a great deal they did not know from the course, for most of those from St. Thomas it opens the door to a whole new world. "I know you will scarcely believe it," a teacher told me, "but some of these children have never seen anything but the sidewalks of Charlotte Amalie. Imagine kids in a place like this having to grow up in what you just have to call an 'asphalt jungle.' " (One St. Thomian student, seeing wild pig tracks on St. John, said, "I didn't know it had elephants in the Virgin Islands National Park.") The new world opened to these town children is already having the desired effect. A *Daily News* reporter told me, "These kids are so hopped up about the environment and ecology that if you drop a gum wrapper in the street, they practically put you under citizen's arrest."

The classes make the trip from St. Thomas to the St. John study area (and also to St. Thomas's Mangrove Lagoon, where some people had wanted to build an airport) by a big white launch, nicely named *Jolly Roger*. I met one such group of more than forty on a hot October morning at Salt Pond Bay as they came ashore loaded with their lunches and water bottles. Mrs. Jadan was with them, having been picked up at Cruz Bay. She and three teachers from St. Thomas shepherded the children along the nature trail. Because of their classroom instruction, some of them recognized the plants and trees and cacti and knew what the salt foam was (I didn't). The walk ended on the rocky shore of Drunk Bay at "Marker 13," a few yards from the water's edge, looking out over the broad Caribbean that stretches unbroken from that point to Venezuela, 600 miles away.

Prevailing winds and currents have deposited on the barren rocks of Drunk Bay the usual debris of the tropical sea: Tree branches, coconuts, shells, battening timbers from ships, and fronds of banana trees. But among the flotsam and jetsam along a 200-yard stretch I walked in this remote place there were a hundred or more plastic containers that had once held detergents, skin lotions, and cleansers—nonbiodegradable material dumped from passing ships and the thousands of pleasure boats used for cruising the "unspoiled Caribbean." There was something else, too. Black gunk, chunks of it everywhere. Mrs. Jadan told me it was congealed petroleum tar. She said that when she first visited Drunk Bay fifteen years ago there was no tar among the rocks. The source of this pollution has not been traced, but it probably comes from oil refineries in Venezuela, Aruba, and elsewhere, and from the tankers that service them (refineries in the Caribbean process more than one hundred million gallons of crude oil daily).

A small St. Thomian came up to show Mrs. Jadan an ugly face he had made with a coconut husk and bits of tar. Another brought a collection of stones and seed pods.

It was impossible on that beach, surrounded by children

who were being taught about their inheritance, not to recognize that the individual *can* do something. But it was also impossible not to think about Hess and Harvey, and the bulldozers and the dredges, and the frenzied efforts to make a lot of money while it still could be made, and to wonder. Who will win? Can the Virgin Islanders, with intelligent cooperation from the federal government, to which they now stand in a new relationship, reverse the ominous course of events in which they have been caught? If not, the Virgins will be truly ruined, and their ruin will create a very serious political and "image" problem for the United States in the Caribbean.

The world beyond the encircling reefs has always threatened the Virgins. Today what happens to the Virgins threatens, by implication and in fact, the world.

Every rape is a diminishment. Rot spreads. No island is an island entire to itself.

Selected Bibliography

ANDERSON, LILLIAN. *Up and Down the Virgin Islands.* Orford, N.H.: Equity Publishing Co. 1963.

AYKROYD, W. R. *Sweet Malefactor: Sugar, Slavery, and Human Society.* London: Heinemann. 1967.

BOUGH, JAMES A., and MACRIDIS, ROY C., eds. *Virgin Islands: America's Caribbean Outpost.* Wakefield, Mass.: Walter F. Williams Publishing Company. 1970.

CAMPBELL, ALFRED A. *St. Thomas Negroes: A Study in Personality and Culture.* Evanston, Ill.: American Psychological Association, Psychological Monographs. Vol. 55, no. 5. 1943.

Catholic Encyclopedia. New York: McGraw-Hill. 1967.

COCHRAN, HAMILTON. *These Are the Virgin Islands.* New York: Prentice-Hall. 1937.

CRASSWELLER, ROBERT D. *The Caribbean Community.* New York: Praeger Publishers. Published for the Council on Foreign Relations. 1972.

CREQUE, DARWIN D. *The U.S. Virgins and the Eastern Caribbean.* Philadelphia: Whitmore Publishing Co. 1968.

EGAN, MAURICE F. *Ten Years Near the German Frontier.* New York: George H. Doran Co. 1919.

EVANS, LUTHER H. *The Virgin Islands from Naval Base to New Deal.* Ann Arbor, Mich.: J. W. Edwards. 1945.

HARMAN, JEANNE. *The Virgins: Magic Islands.* New York: Appleton-Century-Crofts. 1961.

HILL, WALDEMAR, SR. *Rise to Recognition.* St. Thomas, V.I.: The author. 1971.

HOLBROOK, SABRA. *The American West Indies.* New York: Meredith Press. 1969.

IRVING, WASHINGTON. *The Life and Voyages of Christopher Columbus,* vols. 1 and 2. New York: G. P. Putnam. 1849.

JADAN, DORIS. *A Guide to the Natural History of St. John.* St. John, V.I.: Virgin Islands Conservation Society. 1971.

JARVIS, J. ANTONIO. *A Brief History of the Virgin Islands.* St. Thomas, V.I.: The Art Shop. 1938.

————. *The Virgin Islands and Their People.* Philadelphia: Dorrance & Co. 1944.

KNOX, JOHN P. *An Historical Account of St. Thomas, W.I.* New York: Charles Scribner. 1852.

LEWISOHN, FLORENCE. *The Romantic History of St. Croix.* Christiansted, V.I.: St. Croix Landmarks Society. 1964.

PARRY, J. H. *Trade and Dominion.* New York: Praeger Publishers. 1971.

———— and SHERLOCK, PHILIP M. *A Short History of the West Indies.* London: Macmillan; New York: St. Martin's Press. 1968.

SHERLOCK, PHILIP M. *West Indies.* London: Thames & Hudson. 1966.

STEELE, ROBERT V. *The First President Johnson.* New York: Murrow. 1968.

TAUSSIG, C. W. *Rum, Romance, and Rebellion.* New York: Milton, Balch & Co. 1928.

TAYLOR, C. E. *Leaflets from the Danish West Indies.* London: The author. 1888. (Westport, Conn.: Negro Universities Press. 1970.)

WEINSTEIN, EDWIN A. *Cultural Aspects of Delusion.* New York: Free Press of Glencoe. 1962.

WESTERGAARD, WALDEMAR C. *The Danish West Indies Under Company Rule.* New York: Macmillan. 1917.

WILLIAMS, ERIC. *From Columbus to Castro: The History of the Caribbean, 1492–1969.* New York: Harper and Row. 1970.

The World Displayed. London: T. Carnan and F. Newberry. 1774.

ZABRISKIE, LUTHER K. *The Virgin Islands of the United States of America.* New York: G. P. Putnam Sons. 1918.

There was a spate of magazine articles about the Virgin Islands published in the period from 1916 to 1936; since that time most of the attention given to the place by periodicals has been related to travel and tourism. The press since World War II has been sporadic in its coverage of the islands and their problems. Anyone wishing to know more about the territory is directed to the many hearings and reports of committees and subcommittees of Congress and to the annual reports of the governors from 1917 to 1970.